Cherokee
Chapbooks

Donald N. Yates

Other Cherokee Chapbooks

Red Man's Origin
Cherokee Clans
A Memoir of Chief Two White Feathers
Echo the Heart
The Big Little Book of Native American Wit and Wisdom

OLD SOULS IN A NEW WORLD

The Secret History of the

Cherokee Indians

Donald N. Yates

Panther's Lodge

PHOENIX

To Teresa
Wife and Soulmate
Ayeli.

CONTENTS

1 THE HOPIS' ELDER WHITE BROTHER

History is nothing but the soul's old wardrobe.
–Heinrich Heine

"ALL the lights in the House of the High Priests of American Anthropology are out; all the doors and windows are shut and securely fastened (they do not sleep with their windows open for fear that a new idea might fly in); we have rung the bell of Reason, we have banged on the door with Logic, we have thrown the gravel of Evidence against their windows; but the only sign of life in the house is an occasional snore of Dogma. We are very much afraid that no one is going to come down and let us into the warm, musty halls where the venerable old ideas are nailed to the walls."

These biting words were penned by Harold Sterling Gladwin in *Men out of Asia*, the famous archeologist's most popular non-technical work. Published in 1947, Gladwin's book presented a maverick view of the peopling of the Americas, identifying five migrations of diverse races including Negrittoes and Austronesians to the New World. Heretically, he placed the first migration as early as 25,000 years ago and argued that the earliest colonists were Australoid.

The reaction of his colleagues in the anthropological establishment was stony silence, tinged with harumphs and pshaws of injured pride. Gladwin illustrated *Men out of Asia* with droll cartoons by Campbell Grant making fun of the sacred keepers of knowledge at the Peabody Museum at Harvard, Carnegie Foundation and Smithsonian Institution. In one, the dean of Southwest and Maya archeology Alfred V. Kidder is depicted as Dr. Phuddy Duddy sitting in academic robes atop a factory whistle sounding the alarm of illogical chronology. In another, a bespectacled Gladwin and his tweedy friend Professor Earnest Hooton of Harvard are shown in the academic doghouse "by request."

The Establishment is still uncomfortable about Gladwin, who died in 1983 after a distinguished career of more than sixty years. Although willing to praise his meticulous fieldwork on the Hohokam at Snaketown and exacting methodologies developed at the research center he founded at Gila Pueblo outside Globe, Arizona, they do not know quite what to say about his conclusions and hypotheses, which grew more adamant toward the end of his life. The destroying angel of unorthodox theories, Stephen Williams of the Peabody Museum, can only think that Gladwin succumbed to his "whimsies" and grew soft-headed in his old age. "I have always regarded *Men Out of Asia*," Williams loftily declares in *Fantastic Archeology*, "as a sort of spoof."

Thomas Mills lived for many years on the Hopi Indian Reservation in Northern Arizona, where he and his mother opened and operated the Cultural Center at Second Mesa. A close friend was White Bear, the traditionalist who helped Frank Waters compile *The Book of the Hopi* in 1963. Mills was on familiar terms with other elders, kiva chiefs and artisans. In 2001, he wrote a little book of his own called *The Truth*. It was an attempt to reconcile some of the conflicting answers he had received from his sources.

How did a desert-dwelling, isolated people know of the earth's spherical shape and rotation in space? What was the long journey in boats from across the sea they spoke of? And who were the Ant People they took refuge with after the destruction of the first, second and third worlds? Eventually, Mills felt he had some answers from Egyptian religion. He came to believe that the Hopi *were* Egyptians, old souls in Native America, charged with the task of praying for the safety of the world. The delicate balance of affairs in human destiny depended on a Hopi prayer feather or *paho*.

Paho seems to be an Egyptian word (*pw*). Embedded in Hopi customs and rituals are apparently many traces of ancient Old World civilizations. I thought of a time several years ago when Hopi elders David Mowa and Ronald Wadsworth came to give a talk at the university where I was teaching. I noticed David preferred to sleep on the floor in our guest room instead of the pullout bed. That was quite Indian, of course, but his act of leaving a crust of bread on the piano bench when he departed was not. This practice is rooted in the ancient Greek religious gesture of offering bread and milk to the household gods in a strange home.

Author Hamilton Tyler noted several Greek customs among the Pueblo Indians. The plinth-like figure of Masaw evokes the armless guardian statues or herms used by the Greeks as boundary markers. Hermes is both god of roads and boundaries and conductor of the dead to the underworld. "A number of students of Pueblo religion," Tyler admitted, "have remarked that it was something like Greek religion." Yet after uncovering astonishing analogies between the two religions, he concluded that "there is no actual connection between these two gods who lived centuries apart and on different sides of the globe."

Other parallels Tyler dismissed which seem compelling to me are: 1) the Zunis' harlequin-like Mudheads or Koyemshi, who arrive across bridges to taunt and harass people at the ceremony, just as did the clowns released on the Sacred Way between Athens and Eleusis at comic festivals (the word Koyemshi seems indeed to be a corruption of the Greek for "comedians," Latin *comici*), 2) Hermes' and Masaw's playing of tricks on other gods, 3) their gift of song, 4) a body of tales about them as thieves, 5) their status as the inventors of firemaking and as fire gods, 6) their common role of leading the host to war and 7) their respective positions as fertility gods.

In addition to these correspondences, I propose there is an echo of a Greek religious rite in the Zunis' Shalako, the ghostly ancestral figure who initiates reentry of the katsinas into the village at the winter solstice. Shalakos are costumed as luminous white armless figures ten feet high, similar in appearance to the Hopi depiction of Masaw. The Zuni Shalako seems to me to evoke the Egyptian god Osiris, a symbol of regeneration often portrayed as a linen-wrapped mummy. During the Shalako ceremony, the Koyemshi act up and poke fun at the spectators. In the Greek ritual, the maenads and bacchae roam around the crowd and feign tearing to pieces beasts and even humans who come in their way. Their counterparts at Zuni rend to bits live mice and rabbits and carry the small creatures about in their mouths.

Egyptians have long been suspected of visiting the shores of America and even planting colonies here. Whether reached by east or west, the other hemisphere was regarded by them as the realm of Osiris, god of the underworld. As explained by Gunnar Thompson:

> From the vantage point of Egypt, the western Atlantic lies on the opposite side of the globe . . . . [Their] expression "inverted

waters" is an accurate description of the western Atlantic, and it confirms Egyptian knowledge of the Earth's spherical shape. Likewise, the realm of Osiris was known as "The Underworld" because it was located beneath Egypt on the spherical Earth ... Between both worlds flowed the "Two-Ways ocean river .... Egyptian mariners traveled west to the realm of Osiris and returned to the Mediterranean via a "two-ways" ocean river [flowing both directions]—the North Atlantic current.

Could the Egyptians have traveled to the realm of Osiris also by crossing the Pacific from Asia?

Excited by the thought that there might be a real connection between the Hopi and Egyptians, I compiled a list of Hopi words that seem to have the same sound and meaning in Egyptian. Nearly all prove to be archaic terms relating to tribal ceremonies and religious history. The Hopi's main language is classified as Uto-Aztecan, a Native American linguistic phylum, but the formation of plurals with –n and –m points to Semitic or Afro-Asiatic affinities. Specialized religious terms in Hopi are relics or intrusions comparable evidently to fossilized words in the "old language" of the Cherokee. Such vocabulary evokes hieratic or priestly languages like Sanskrit in India or Latin in Western Europe.

With this daring key, events recounted in *The Book of the Hopi* became crystal-clear. Of the various former world ages or epochs recalled by the Hopi, one of them, Kuskurza, is specifically said to be "an ancient name for which there is no modern meaning." Reading the names of these epochs in Ancient Egyptian gives them true significance. They are: 1) World Destroyed by Fire (Tokpela), 2) Time Long Ago (Tokpa), 3) Age of Abandon (Kuzkurza), and 4) Age of the Strangers from Afar, the Fourth World or Present (Tuwaqachi). Thus, the creator Taiowa (Uto-Aztecan or Tanoan for "man, human, people," as in today's Tewa, Tiwa and Towa) has his nephew Sotuknang and Spider Woman give life to the innocent First People in an Eden called Tokpela. They are led astray by the Talker and Katoya the handsome one (Satan the deceiver). The animals draw apart in fear and they begin to fight one another, in neglect of the Creator's plan. Sotuknang decides to annihilate the world by opening up the volcanoes and raining fire upon it, but not before saving some of the faithful by leading them to a big mound where the Ant People live. The Egyptian word for this refuge the Hopi will use to survive two further holocausts translates literally as "subsistence in the pyramid of the ants." Pyramid, in fact, means "anthill."

After the end of Tokpela, World Destroyed by Fire, the people emerge to the Second World, called Dark Midnight, but they begin to become preoccupied with materialistic concerns as before. They ignore once again the commandments of the Creator. Sotuknang and Spider Woman seal a select few in the underground world of the Ant People and direct the celestial Twins to leave their posts at the north and south poles. The earth spins around off its axis, rolls over twice and freezes into solid ice. After it warms and the earth and seas are revived, Sotuknang brings the remnants of mankind out of the Ant kiva to emerge into the third world, Kuskurza.

True to its name, Kuskurza is full of big cities, jewels, copper, tobacco and speeding vessels called *patuwvota*. The Bow Clan behind these marvels corrupts everybody with wickedness until finally Sotuknang and Spider Woman intervene and put an end to the Age of Abandon with a devastating flood. This time the faithful are loaded onto reed boats. Spider Woman guides them to the Fourth World (Age of the Strangers from Afar). They dwell in stages on a succession of islands and continue to travel toward the northeast until they reach the new Place of Emergence. Hopi elders believe this to have been the coast of California, but it may have been at the mouth of the Colorado River on the Sea of Cortez, for the Hopi enact a coming-of-age ritual each year by sending youths on a footrace to collect salt here from a site associated with their ancestors. In former times, there were several large inland seas and the river system of the region was different.

> Looking to the west and the south, the people could see sticking out the water the islands upon which they had rested.
>
> "They are the footprints of your journey," continued Sotuknang, "the tops of the high mountains of the Third World, which I destroyed. Now watch."
>
> As the people watched them, the closest one sank under the water, then the next, until all were gone, and they could see only water.
>
> "See," said Sotuknang, "I have washed away even the footprints of your Emergence, the stepping-stones which I left for you. Down on the bottom of the seas lie all the proud cities, the flying *pátuwvotas*, and the worldly treasures

corrupted with evil, and those people who found no time to sing praises to the Creator from the tops of their hills."

Once the people make landfall in their new home, the old gods Sotuknang and Spider Woman depart and leave the emergent Hopi to their own devices. This is a clue to the origin of this cosmic tale, which must have arisen in Sundaland, or Island Indonesia, among what the Cherokee called the "wise ones of Seg." Indeed, throughout the entire Southwest Pacific Ocean, cosmologies focus on the figures of the Father Sky (Sotuknang) and Earth Mother (Spider Woman), the former usually portrayed as warlike and destructive, the latter as the creator of all the arts of civilization that sustain and nourish the people, as, for instance, weaving, basket-making and agriculture.

The central role of the Spider as the helper of mankind is preserved in two Cherokee tales. In one, Grandmother Spider Steals the Sun, it is the tiny water spider who swims across the water to an island where the fire burns in order to bring warmth and comfort to her freezing people. In another, the same water spider dives deep under the waves to bring up dirt and form the new country inhabited by the people.

We may therefore best understand *The Book of the Hopi* as codifying a sweeping vision of world history created by a founder civilization that came from Eden in the East (to use Stephen Oppenheimer's term). In the mythic underpinnings of this society, there had been an age of man destroyed by volcanic eruptions (Tokpela) followed by global darkness, undoubtedly the fallout of such a cataclysm (Tokpa, the Second World). This age, too, is destroyed, this time by ice, with the Celestial Twins forsaking their axes: Scientists today acknowledge the effect of the poles in causing Ice Ages. Kurskurza, the Third World of Abandon, ensues after the melting of the ice, but it quickly ends in floods. Its trademark is the boat (*patuwvota*). The old worlds having been destroyed by fire, by icy darkness and by rising waters, the survivors make their way to the Fourth, and Present, World, where they are called, in Egyptian, the People from Foreign Lands. Hohokam, the name of the Southwest's "mother civilization," means People from the Sea in Ancient Egyptian. From this, we may surmise that Egyptian boats made of reed conveyed the Islanders to their new home.

There the people meet Masaw, who becomes their guardian and protector. He is described as black and ugly, scratching out a humble existence in Oraibi ("Cliff Town" in ancient Greek) on Second Mesa.

He declines to be their leader but gives them permission to stay. First, however, they must start their migrations to the ends of the earth (*paso*, another Egyptian word).

The name Masaw is the same as Ancient Egyptian *msw* "Libyan." The Hopi say Oraibi was his original home, which they translate as Rock on High, but which is formed apparently from a Greek word meaning "boundary, landmark, covenant stone." Inasmuch as "fire" has the sense of "a group of Indian people," their discovery of Masaw sitting with his back to them around a fire implies not just one black man or Libyan but a nation of them. Another Second Mesa town, Shungnopavi, is translated as Place of the Black Man, although in Egyptian it means "fertile land, field of reeds," this being the main metaphor in their religion for the afterlife, or paradise. That these Libyans were of the same stock as ancient soldiers and mariners from the Old World is supported by the fact that a later character in *The Book of the Hopi*, Horny Toad Woman, tells Masaw, "I too have a metal helmet," in other words, armor.

The various names of the Hopi are also informative. These are Hoki, the secret original ethnonym, which seems to come from the Egyptian word for "magicians"; Hopi, the Peaceful Ones, Egyptian for "people of the law"; and Moqui, erroneously glossed as neighboring tribes' derogatory reference to them as "despicable people." In actuality Moqui is probably derived from Magi.

Aside from Oraibi, another trace of the Greek language comes to us from Acoma. A legend there tells of the arrival of its first inhabitants. The story goes that there once lived a boy all by himself on Enchanted Mesa. One day he heard the shouts of a strange people. A town was founded in the spot where the echo was heard. The word Acoma is garbled Spanish, but in the Acoma language Haku'uw is very close to the Greek word *echo*, related to English "acoustic."

If Acoma has a hint of Greek, Zuni is pure Libyan. Its very form Ashiwi refers to the Oasis of Siwa in the land the ancients called Ammonia after its patron god of the sun, Ammon. Barry Fell sees the Zuni language as having "a large Libyo-Egyptian element similar to Coptic, to which have been added Ptolemaic roots brought to the Egyptian and Libyan lands by Greek settlers in the wake of the Spartan colonization of Libya in the eight century B.C. and the conquest of Egypt by . . . the Ptolemies, during the last four centuries B.C." There are also roots of Nilotic origin, he adds, introduced by Nubian slaves—perhaps a reason why the Zunis traditionally divide themselves into a red and black half in their village. Zuni religion owes much to the worship of Ammon as practiced in the land of Ammonia with its capital of Siwa.

An early observer of the Zuni, Herman Ten Kate, found the tribe to "have been familiar with the art of silversmithing for some time" and highly skilled at polishing shells and turquoise to make necklaces. Moreover, they "surpass all other North American tribes in making of pottery," especially large ollas for holding water. Their painting was black on while and their decorations ran to meanders, spirals and wavy lines, he said.

Other signs of Zuni's Old World origins are found in the name of its priesthood, Shi'wanikwe ("people of Siwa") and the place-name of an outlying village where apparently the Canaanite element among them settled, Kia'anaän. The Zunis' tribal name is Children of the Sun. Ten Kate notes, "In addition to their everyday spoken language, the Zunis have a more ancient language, known only to the highest priests, in which the prayers of their order are recited." He also reports that in Zuni traditions their ancestors came from the West in boats:

> That they were aware of the sea during their earlier wanderings seems to be the case not only because they worship it but because they are at the same time familiar with the octopus or one of the other cephalopods . . . . Through tradition they are also familiar with earthquakes. They are labeled with the name of "the sound from the shell of the gods" . . . the tradition in this respect refers to how "the ocean was whipped to a fury" by "the sound of the shell of the gods." Moreover, in former times they undertook pilgrimages to the coast of the Pacific Ocean for the purpose of collecting sacred shells . . . just as the Moquis [Hopis] did.

In Greek mythology, Poseidon, the god of oceans, creates earthquakes. Triton, a fish-tailed demigod worshiped in particular in Cyrene, blows the conch trumpet that controls the waves and sounds the approach of an earthquake. It is hard to imagine a better set of clues.

Libyan settlement in North America is apparent from North African writing systems, building styles and languages. The evidence for it ranges from a famous *tholos*-shaped subterranean stone chamber in Upton, Massachusetts to pre-alphabetic writing in a stick-script called ogam scattered across the American West. Inscriptions in ogam, Greek, Kufic Arabic, Phoenician, Tifanag (a Berber alphabet), Celto-

Iberian and Egyptian all point to the Libyans. Many of the remains of the mixed Berber/Semitic/Greek/Egyptian peoples in the rock record have been identified and deciphered but many more have been overlooked or explained away. The monumental New England beehive chambers Fell believed to be in the style of Berber kivas were dismissed as colonial root cellars!

In 1994, Gloria Farley, an epigrapher, published the results of nearly fifty years of exploration in and around her native state of Oklahoma. The massive book was titled *In Plain Sight;* a second volume was anticipated at the time of her death in 2006. *In Plain Sight* provides a good look at these Native Americans who were not who they were supposed to be, who used metal when they ought to have been still in the Stone Age, and who had writing despite the denial of it to them by modern-day anthropology. Chapter titles tell it all: They Came in Ships. . . They Signed Their Names . . . They Claimed the Land . . . The Trail of the Egyptians . . . They Knew the Sky . . . They Mourned Their Dead.

When my wife and I first moved to New Mexico, we immediately paid a visit to Bandelier National Archeological Monument twelve miles southeast of Los Alamos. The general impression it gives is a Greek, Roman or Tunisian site. How did the people who lived here hew all those blocks of sandstone, slate, and even granite and basalt? Tens of thousands of squared-off stones were required to build Bandelier, and hundreds, if not thousands, of metal tools. "Obsidian," the ranger told us. But obsidian shatters on stone. Nor can stone be used to chop stone: An archeological experiment attempting to do this produced an eighty percent degradation of tools within a few hours. And as though this were not enough, after being pointed out the path to what the ranger called Quetzalcoatl's Cave, we stood face to face with a deeply incised example of ogam. Peeking into a cliff-dwelling down the way, we saw Tifanag writing in a painted plaster ceiling.

Ogam has been recognized in Celtic lands for several centuries, but it was Barry Fell who first studied its remote origins. A seminal document is the short Ogam Tract added to the end of a medieval Irish manuscript kept today in the library of Trinity College, Dublin. This treatise in the great Book of Ballymote contains specimens of ogam arranged geographically with Gaelic and Latin translations beside them. Its rediscovery proved to be the Rosetta Stone for ancient North African writing. Fell was able through this link to decipher different versions in Libyan, Egyptian, Punic, Ibero-Celtic and a welter of other languages. For instance, a script called African by the Ballymote scribe is an Iberian variety used by Semitic speakers in southern Spain during the first millennium B.C.E. Fell published a chart comparing the oldest styles with the fully developed and more familiar Irish style of the Middle Ages.

Predictably, his discoveries were ridiculed. Archeology students today are still cautioned by their professors not to cite *anything* that appears to be prehistoric writing in America. Ever since Major Powell directed the Smithsonian's Bureau of Ethnology, there has been an academic ban on such reckless speculation.

I was not surprised to discover upon my return to Santa Fe that among the hundreds of books, surveys and dissertations written about Bandelier, not one mention was made of the marks on the rock-face outside Quetzalcoatl's Cave. One of my friends suggested it was a place where the Bandelierian Indians sharpened their arrows.

The Bandelier inscription is a textbook case of Old Ogam and unquestionably was produced with the aid of metal tools. From right to left in the fashion of Hebrew, it reads: Q-H-T-Z-H-L C-TL-H-TL-H. The marks are in a style similar to a specimen discovered on Manana Island, near Monhegan Island on the coast of Maine. Sometimes called Hinged Ogam, this is a variety of Bronze Age ogam quite common in America, corresponding roughly to no. 16 in the Irish Ogam Tract. The Manana stone states: "Ships from Phoenicia, Cargo platform."

There *are* images of Quetzalcoatl in the rock art record of the American Southwest, quite a few actually, although only a small number have been adequately elucidated. Crosses are signs of his cult, just as the face or mask represents him in his aspect of god of life and death. Interestingly, this Feathered Serpent's final resting place (if that is what it is) forms a rock cavity or catacomb similar to those carved by ancient Phoenicians and Libyan peoples. The cult of the dead, especially of entombed kings and saints, still exists among the modern Berbers in the practices of Maraboutism.

Like the god Pan in ancient Greece, Quetzalcoatl is unique for having both a birth and death. He first appears as a culture-bearer in a ship arriving from the East, bearded, clad all in white and wearing a distinctive conical hat. Later, he is identified with the son of the Toltec emperor Mixcoatl. Beginning in the seventh century the Toltecs were ruled for nine generations by priest-kings with the name Quetzalcoatl. The first of these was honored for having overturned the practice of human sacrifice (a religious rite of the Phoenicians) but later he was assassinated by enemies opposed to his reforms. In another myth, Quetzalcoatl sails off toward the rising sun, promising one day to return. In Yucatan he is called Kukulcan. Moctezuma, the Aztec emperor of Mexico at the time of the Spanish conquest, was well versed in the prophecies about Quetzalcoatl and thought the foreigners to be the returning white gods of legend.

The so-called Jornada Style of rock art and pottery decoration in the Southwest includes numerous representations of Quetzalcoatl, as well as another important Mesoamerican figure, Tlaloc (pronounced Choc), the goggle-eyed rain god. Tlaloc is thought to be the chief deity represented in Hopi and Pueblo katsinas, the rain-bringer who once demanded human sacrifice (those Phoenicians again). Quetzalcoatl is affiliated with fish, travel, trade, agriculture and fertility.

Quetzalcoatl becomes the Horned or Plumed Water Serpent of the Pueblo Indians, patron of rivers, springs and irrigation. He is recognizable in the Hopi Sky God, who wears a single horn or high cone when masked and hat shaped like a star when unmasked. The mask is another emblem associated with these foreign gods. In their katsina rain-bringing rituals, Hopi and other Pueblo Indians incorporate both masks and crosses.

Through these correspondences, a historical overlay of Mexican religion on the Hopis' original Egyptian and Greek culture begins to crystallize. Quetzalcoatl replaces Osiris and fulfills the same purpose of resurrection and bringing of the rains and floods for crops. In Hopi spirituality, Osiris transforms into Masaw. Both are gods of the underworld and judges of the dead. One of the most familiar scenes in Egyptian religion, shown repeatedly in copies of the Book of the Dead, was Osiris' weighing of the deceased person's heart. The heart is ideally balanced by his prayers in the shape of a feather—the origin of our expression "light-hearted." Entry into the afterlife is guarded by Osiris in the form of a mummy—one with the uncanny likeness of Masaw. The deceased's soul (*ka*) embarks on the reed ship of the Sun to the underworld much as the Hopis travel also in reed boats to reach the other side of the world. Like a resurrected Egyptian in the Elysian Fields, the devout Hopi is rewarded by ample rains, fertile, fruitful fields and an eternity of plenitude. Hopi cloud terraces are the same as the Egyptian staircase to heaven. The water birds (*benu* in Egyptian, "phoenix") and other symbols of the Nile in its aspect of constant renewal are reflected in Hopi pottery designs, as are multitudinous other elements of Egyptian religion.

What, then, is to be made of Kokopelli, the hump-backed flute-player so pervasive in Southwestern Indian art?

Chaco Canyon is a complex of ruins on the other side of the Jemez Mountains from Bandelier. Like Bandelier, it is seen as a part of Ancestral Pueblo history and assigned to between about 1000 and 1250 C.E. Lying at a latitude of 36° N, longitude 108° W, with an elevation exactly one mile high, its bone-dry red rock canyon falls in the center of the San Juan River drainage area. Chaco Wash is a deeply etched *arroyo* that flows only after heavy rains. When these occur, water jets down the walls of the mesa into the village. The growing season is short, always less than 150 days and often less than 100 days—not a productive place for corn. Wood resources are scarce, and the surrounding desert exhibits only the rare clump of pygmy juniper or rabbitbush. According to archeologists, climate in the centuries when Chaco Culture flourished was not much different.

So what is it doing here?

Following the circuit road one first comes to the Great House or outlying apartment building of Hungo Pavi (Reed Spring). The name is thought to be the same as Shungopavi, one of the mother villages of the Hopi on Second Mesa, a name we can now derive from Ancient Egyptian *hni* "rush" and *pw* "it is." Next on the visitors route is the elevated Great Kiva of Chetro Ketl (a Navajo corruption of Quetzalcoatl?). After that comes Pueblo Bonita, a ruin of 700 rooms within D-shaped perimeter walls up to three stories high. Sighting down a long ceremonial avenue leading back to Hungo Pavi one cannot but be struck by the distant silouette of a giant figure formed by the shadows in the cliff. One hundred feet tall, it appears to be Kokopelli, complete with hunch, flute, and triangular hat or horn.

Chaco may have been built where it was, and how it was, because of the striking shadows on its canyon walls. Certainly, the choice of location owes much to the Libyans with their cliff-dwelling habits and knowledge of irrigation. Kokopelli like Quetzalcoatl is a rain-bringer, culture bearer and peddler or merchant. The gates, walls and sight lines of Pueblo Bonita emphasize view of the city's patron saint.

Cosmopolitan Chaco lasted perhaps little over six decades in the eleventh century, with successor sites at Aztec Ruins to the north and Casas Grandes in the south ending a bit later. After the Pueblo Indians had shaken off its autocratic rulers, they retained memories of Chaco as a dark place, ruled by "a people who had enormous amounts of power: spiritual power and power over people." The shadows of Chaco Canyon were responsible for a determined democracy in tribal affairs ever afterwards. The reason Kokopelli is often shown in a recumbent position in petroglyphs is not because he is in bed, but because he is dead.

Impelled by years of drought, civil and political turmoil and invasions by Athabaskan and Aztec hordes from the north, the Hopi returned to Oraibi and the three mesas where they are now located in the fourteenth century. The earliest date for Old Oraibi as established by tree ring chronology performed on its wooden timbers is 1150 C.E. Elders quoted in *The Book of the Hopi* speak of the 1200s and 1300s as a time when other groups such as the Badger Clan were gathered in after petitioning for admittance. They say that the Navajos and Apaches did not arrive in Hopi territory until one generation before the Spanish (1580).

Enter now the Elder White Brother.

According to tradition, Masaw gave the Hopi four tablets to safeguard as their original instructions. The Sun Clan tablet applies primarily to the members of that clan. The Hopi are mostly silent about the symbols on it but they insist that a now-lost Elder White Brother was given a corner and charged with returning after being sent to the East.

I believe the headless person they interpret as a wicked chief beheaded as a warning not to disobey their covenant is not that at all. In ancient Libya, rulers were buried without their heads; it was a sign of royalty and even divine status. Surely, this is a depiction of a Libyan expedition's leader or governor. Note that the figure is within a cartouche, the shape reserved for a pharaoh's name. The inscriptions on the tablet could probably be read as Numidian by an expert in that script (which I am not).

In ancient times, a bargain or promise was sealed by breaking a tablet, stick or other object so that a later match between the two parts would identify the rightful partners when the contract was fulfilled. Elder Brother was sent with instructions to look for the missing members of the original migration, those whom history would know as the Cherokee. We lose track of them somewhere about Oklahoma.

Among the unusual finds Gloria Farley describes in her book *In Plain Sight* is a stone pulled out of the family's farmland by curious eleven-year-old Brent Gorman of Warner, Oklahoma, in 1971. It was identified by Barry Fell as a Libyan boundary stone in the Numidian alphabet. His translation of its script, which resembles that of the Sun Clan tablet, was: Land Belonging to Rata. A discussion of the Warner Stone was published in Fell's book *America B.C.* and its Numidian writing system and the interpretation of the latter were confirmed by visits from surprised scholars at the Universities of Tripoli and Benghazi in Libya. The stone is now in the permanent collection of the Kerr Museum in Poteau, Oklahoma.

John RedHat Duke (1930-2002) was a Cherokee elder enrolled both with the United Keetoowah Band and Cherokee Nation of Oklahoma. A member also of the Keetoowah Society, he converted to Judaism as a teen-ager and became a Levite priest, making his *aliyah* and achieving Israeli citizenship under the "Law of Return."

Both full-blood grandmothers spoke the old Southern Keetoowah dialect. He was a strong believer in the Lost Tribes of Israel theory of American Indian origins.

RedHat came to the attention of Hopi Elders at Oraibi in the 1960s because he apparently fulfilled Hopi prophecy, which stated that one day the True White Brother would arrive from the largest Indian nation bringing a new religion from the east and wearing a red hat or cloak. The Cherokee are the most populous Indian nation, and they are located east of the Hopi. The last *kykmongwe*, or high chief, Mike Lansa, declared the prophecy fulfilled except for one detail. The Bahana was to return the missing corner of the Sun Clan tablet, which John Duke failed to do.

2 SECRET OF THE KEETOOWAH PRIESTS

Nice contradiction between fact and fact
Will make the whole read human and exact.
—Robert Graves, "The Devil's Advice to Story-tellers"

DON'T the Cherokee have a creation story like the Hopi in Arizona, Algonquian tribes or other American Indians? Don't they have a uniform mythology similar to the Romans, Greeks and British with their traditional epic foundation stories or, for that matter, Americans with their tales of the Pilgrims and Lexington and Concord and Declaration of Independence? As it turns out, the answer to this question is yes, they do.

The secret of the Cherokees has been placed right in front of us all the time, and in fact, published. It is widely known that the Cherokees had writing with the so-called Sequoyan syllabary, that they were literate from an early period of their existence. What is not well known is that they had schools, learned societies, oral traditions transmitted from generation to generation and even universities. At a time when most of the country lacked public schools and universal schooling requirements for children, the Cherokee built colonnaded brick campuses for males and females in the scrub hills of Indian Territory. Since the 1820s, the Cherokee have maintained bilingual newspapers published in their own language and unique syllabary.

In 1880, the Cherokees of Oklahoma received their first full-fledged institution of higher education when the American Baptist Home Mission Society started Indian University in Tahlequah.

Renamed Bacone University, it eventually developed a press. One of the press's first publications was a slender little octavo-sized book titled *A Cherokee Vision of Eloh'*. Based on a report in the newspaper *Indian Chieftain* by Cornsilk (Cherokee name of William Eubanks), and rendering the deposition of Sakiyah Sanders, a member of the secret priestly society of the Keetoowahs in the 1890s, this Cherokee History of the World, as the original title may be literally translated, tells of a unique "heritage of history, spirituality and prophecy . . . in a matter sensitive to native understanding." The document narrates in Cherokee and English on facing pages the story of the travels of twelve original clans to North America across a large western body of water that can only be the Pacific Ocean. They migrate to escape overcrowding and frequent floods in the old country. Before leaving, the Cherokees, whom the document names Eshelokee, build a "store reaching to heaven," but this is destroyed "by the gods."

According to the Keetoowah text, "Other red tribes or clans to the Cherokee tribe began to come also from the old country," and:

> . . . in the course of time the old pathway which had been traveled by the clans was cut [broken] by the submergence of a portion of the land into the deep sea. This path can be traced to this day by the broken boulders. This was of no surprise to the clans as they were used to the workings of the floods.

For many years after establishing their new homes, the settlers search for the missing five clans. Unable to find them, they "gave it up and established a new system of seven sacred clans to the tribe. From that day to this[,] they have been searching for the five lost clans of the Cherokee." At some point in the Eshelokee's wanderings, it is not clear when, or where, "a black race of terrible invaders came in boats over the sea." The first wave is repulsed by the Cherokee warriors, as are "thousands upon thousands" of them, until the Cherokees discover the poison of a dragon, the dread Uktena, to kill them and prevent any further irruptions. After that, they live "for ages" in peace, and "knowledge of the war with the dark invader became in the course of time only a story."

Brian Wilkes, an expert on the Cherokee language and traditions, says there were four invasions of the old land, called Elohi Mona in song. On the fourth invasion, the Cherokees used the monstrous Uktena's venom but in so doing contaminated the land and rendered it unfit for habitation. The poison destroyed the invaders, but the land was so devastated it soon afterward "sank into the ocean." Such a chain of events could well pass today for a fable of environmental disaster.

The rest of the text describes the coming of Europeans, whom the Cherokee welcome at first but soon discover to be a "race of deceit and cunning." Christianity is called "the writing of a strange teaching that the white invader claimed to have spoken from heaven[,] the truth or untruth of which the red tribe had to find out for themselves." Notably, there are multiple waves of white people landing in North America in this version of history, suggesting a much deeper time frame than 1492, the date most of us are fixated on for entry of Europeans into the Americas. Twelve divisions of the Eshelokee are presented. It is likely that the Cherokee clans came from different homelands in the "old country." According to tradition, their seven clans reflect occupational castes of warriors, foragers, hunters, builders, healers, priests and messenger-diplomats.

As for the floods in the Keetoowah origin story, these details agree with the ancestral homeland of the Cherokees described in their ritual recitation at the green-corn dance, where keepers of sacred stories performed enormous feats of memory annually with the help of wampum belts for the benefit of the young people. This origin-place of the Cherokees contained great snakes and water monsters, "for which reason it was supposed to have been near the seacoast" according to anthropologists. Another Cherokee tradition, similar to the Hopis', tells of a single devastating flood triggered by earthquakes.

The Keetoowah text mentions a "store reaching to heaven," destroyed in the old homeland. The Tower of Babel myth, as has been revealed by recent ethnographic research, goes far beyond Mesopotamia and the Fertile Crescent. It has roots in the Far East. Oxford genetics professor Stephen Oppenheimer derives tales of a primordial tower built in defiance of heaven from a civilization situated east of India and even Burma, evidently an Austronesian one. In the Keetoowah account we are told of invasions by a fierce race of black men. This detail seems puzzling at first since, according to Cornsilk (or Sanders), the Cherokee's lost ancestral home lies beyond the western shores of the Pacific Ocean. Although called dark, and black, the invaders do not seem to be Africans. They are said to come from the west. They arrive by sea.

In this Cherokee religious narrative, we read that "the ancient worship of the wise ones of heaven," was brought over from the old country "beyond memory" and "reorganized in the new country

[America] as the ancient religion." Once the last wave of invaders, the white men, gain a foothold and begin dispossessing them of their land, the Cherokee are ultimately "driven to the seashore [of the West Coast], where they will cross the waters[;] . . . landing in the old country from when[ce] they came." There, they "will find the five lost clans, became [sic] reunited into twelve clans, into one people again, will become a great nation known as the Eshelokee of the half-sphere temple of light."

A word that leaps from the page in this strange account is *cahtiyis*, the "half-sphere temple of light," glossed as "possibly a reference to town house." It is left in its original language, whatever that might be. Obviously it was an enigma to the Cherokee editors. *Cahtiyis* provides an important and authentic clue to the origins of these seaborne migrants with their institutions of multiple gods, temples, flags and council houses. If *cahtiyis* is a foreign word, as it appears to be, what language does it come from? Suggestively, almost letter for letter, it is Doric Greek. The literal meaning is "a sitting down," which fits well in the context of the Keetoowah text. It is the standard Greek name for an assembly hall. These public buildings were often constructed in a circular shape to emphasize egalitarian principles. The assembled citizenry, arranged by tribe and clan, sometimes reclined on bench-like couches or rafters as do many American Indians even today (and as do Jews once a year when celebrating a Seder).

The word applies well to a rotund style of architecture whose social function as a dome-shaped place of worship evokes the Southwestern American Indian kiva as well as the Cherokee council house familiar to us from eighteenth-century travelers' accounts.

The use of columns is especially telling, as is the forthright use of the word "temple." The Doric Greek architecture of the *tholos* seems pertinent here. In its classic shape, the *tholos* consisted of a circular drum of columns covered by a parasol-shaped roof supported by internal wooden posts. The form also appears in tombs and is notable in the monumental national architecture of Washington, D.C.

An important part of the ceremonies conducted in both the Cherokee council house and temples of Apollo was to introduce young men who had come of age in the intervening year into the community to take their rightful position in their clan, phratry (fraternity), military unit, priesthood or other social division. The same function was, and is, fulfilled each year in the Southwestern Indian kiva.

Although called a heptagon, the Cherokee national assembly hall was seven-sided only in a figurative sense. In actuality it was octagonal. Inside, along the eighth wall in front sat the "peace" or White Chief and "war" or Red Chief flanked by assistants and counselors with a screen separating the public or profane space from the sacred area or inner sanctum behind them. The medicine bundle, or "ark of the nation," was kept here in the same way as the Ark of the Covenant was concealed in the Holy of Holies in the Temple in Jerusalem, or as the religious paraphernalia of gods and goddesses were hidden from common view in the cella of a Greek temple. In the Cherokee "temple," there was a flag outside the narrow entrance portico and painted standards with calendrical symbols of the sun and moon attached to the posts inside.

Along with *cahtiyis*, the "half-sphere temple of light," the word Eloh' may also have Greek roots. Cognate with the Doric *alaan* ("be driven"), *Eloi* can be taken to signify "wanderers." Homer, whose works were learned by rote by schoolchildren and who was often quoted in the ancient world, uses the related word *ala* of Odysseus' wandering or roaming without home or hope of rest. This interpretation fits with the name of the ancestral land in Cherokee legends, Elohi Mona, for Mona can also be read as strict Doric Greek: *mona*, "abiding place, a place to stay in." Hence the name preserved in Cherokee song seems to mean Place Where the Wanderers Tarried.

Could the other untranslated word in the treatise, Eshelokee, also be Greek? The author recalls a remark by Paul Russell, a Potawatomi-Shawnee-Cherokee elder who was one of his teachers: "Nobody really knows where the name Tsalagi [pronounced Cha-la-kee] comes from. It's odd that the Tsalagi Warrior Society always pronounces it Shalokee, with an *s* and *h*." Members of the Warrior Society, which still flourishes in parts of Tennessee and North Carolina, distinguish themselves in this way from the overarching tribe, the Tsalagi, with its *ts* sound.

Eshelokee, which specifically refers to the warrior caste and is, after all, the foundation of *Vision of the Elohi*, is the same word as Greek *etheloikeoi*, "willing settlers, colonizers." The *th* sound of the Greek is replaced by an *sh* sound. Cherokee like many Native American languages has no exact equivalent to a *th* sound. Eshelokee is evidently a proper name for those who joined the travels across the face of the earth or Elohi—the crew members, conscripts and other members of an expedition. Such a derivation may explain why the customary name for the Cherokee—Tsalagi—famously resists all efforts to etymologize it. In the form *choloki*, according to anthropologists, it designates "people of foreign speech." This common explanation rests on a lingua franca of the Southeastern Indians called Choctaw trade jargon. But that interpretation begs a question. There are other etymologies, although none is capable of being analyzed into elements of the Cherokee language.

According to the author of a recent grammatical study of Oklahoma Cherokee, Brad Montgomery-Anderson, "There are several beliefs about the origin of the name *jalagi*, but it appears that the word itself is not a native Cherokee word." The names used for Cherokee people by their neighbors and surrounding Indian nations vary widely. The Seneca and other northern tribes call them "cave people" (*Oyatakea*), others, "record keepers," still others, including themselves, "dog people."

Currently, Cherokee is spoken as their primary language by fewer than a hundred human beings on the planet, nearly all of them rural Oklahomans well advanced in years. Most people if asked today would probably take the position, as do linguists, that it is "the sole representative of the Southern branch of the Iroquoian family of languages."

If, however, as the linguists believe, Cherokee split off from a proto-Iroquoian language at a distant remove in time equal about to the divide that separates descendants of Swiss or Bavarian Low German from standard High German, or Czech from Polish, or French from Provençal, disturbing questions arise about the relationship of Cherokee and other Iroquoian languages. Why are the two languages not mutually intelligible? A Cherokee speaker has the same odds of being understood by a Haudenosaunee or Mohawk speaker as a Russian by a Vietnamese or Anglo-Saxon warlord by a BBC newscaster. Why does Mohawk have two or three times as many words as Cherokee? Why does Cherokee have a radically different syntax and grammar from Mohawk? Compared to Mohawk, Cherokee is so stripped bare and simple it comes across as pidgin English. Could that simplicity be illusory? Are we misled by the fact that it is spoken so poorly now as a second language? Why is two-thirds of its vocabulary non-cognate, not sharing the same roots as Mohawk? The lack of overlap extends to basic words like the names of numbers. In Mohawk, seven is *tsjada*. In Cherokee it is *gahlgwogi*.

Could the original Cherokee, the Eshelokee, have spoken a non-Indian language, and might it have been a form of Greek? According to our informant Brian Wilkes, before they relocated to the Smoky Mountains, the Cherokees lived for generations in the Ohio Valley. Here they quarreled with the Iroquoian people, who had been their allies and fellow travelers in recent migrations. To resolve that conflict, it was decided it would be easier for the Cherokees to learn the local tongue Mohawk than for the Iroquois to switch to the difficult language the Cherokees spoke. Since that time, the Cherokees have spoken a form of Iroquoian.

Wilkes goes on to say that "when the conflicts arose again, the Cherokees and their close relations the Tuscaroras went south, the Cherokees settling in the Mountains and the Tuscaroras settling closer to the coast. After clashing with the English, the Tuscarora returned north in 1718, becoming the sixth nation of the Haudenosaunee [Iroquois Confederacy]. The Cherokees were also invited to return, but history sent them in a different direction.

Some say the old language was similar to Hopi, Wilkes adds, and that the Cherokees who went east after forking off from the main group in Arkansas are the Bahana or Elder White Brother of Hopi prophecy. Others say the discarded language is Mayan, and the Cherokee are the *Chan,* the Snake People (boat builders) who went north, according to Maya elders. "Boat people" refers to their origins as seafarers because Chan means both "snake" and "canoe, boat." This compelling if untidy account is supported by the linguistic relationship of the Cherokee, Tuscarora and Iroquois; by the immediate provenance of the Cherokee from the Ohio Valley; by the traditional enmity between the Iroquois and Cherokee; and by certain connections between the Hopi, Cherokee, Maya and Incas.

At any rate, it is clear that a substantial number of Cherokee words are of foreign extraction. Similarly, several of the details of the Eshelokee origin-story evoke similar ones in the mythology of people on the other side of the world. Take the Uktena, for example, the dragon whose venom allows the Cherokee to repulse the foreign black invaders before its poison pollutes the land. This word makes perfect sense in the Greek language. It cannot be analyzed into Cherokee elements—a failing which suggests foreign roots. It probably derives from *ou* "not" and *ktennais* "slain." The literal meaning is Unslayable One.

Significant hints about the solution to the Cherokee "enigma," as Cyclone Covey called it, come from Cyrene. After long study, I am persuaded that the Wanderers described in the Vision of Elohi most likely originated in this important Doric-speaking colony of Sparta, modern Shahat in Libya. Spartans were transplanted there en masse following their defeat in the Peloponnesian War of 431-405 B.C.E. Cyrene had been founded by Dorian Greeks from the island of Thera, modern-day Santorini, near Crete, and owed its first cultural influences to the Minoans, who ruled Thera until the devastating volcanic eruption of 1650-1500 B.C.E. Cyrene and the surrounding area flourished for nearly a thousand years, first as a kingdom, briefly as a republic, then as a city-state or polis within the domain of Carthage. Under the Ptolemies it was an allied client state of Egypt; its port of Apollonia was second only to Alexandria, the Ptolemaic capital. Finally, it became the Roman province of Cyrenaica. The Romans reunited it with Crete, bringing its history full circle. Importantly, Cyrene was the chief cult city of Apollo. Apollo's temple there was the most famous shrine of the sun-god in the ancient world.

With a population of 135,000 people, Cyrenaica was home to one of the largest and most prosperous Jewish communities outside ancient Israel. It was surpassed only by Alexandria, the Egyptian capital and greatest merchant port of its day. At this time Jews were thoroughly Hellenized. They not only spoke Greek as their first language, even at the High Temple in Jerusalem, but had adopted customs such as play-going, athletics and public baths. Judaism had absorbed many elements of pagan Greek and Egyptian religion.

Classical scholar Shimon Appelbaum, an authority on ancient Cyrene, estimates 5,000 Jews lived in the capital city. The Roman Jewish historian Josephus says they enjoyed equal rights before the law with other inhabitants. The country adopted a progressive form of government as early as the fifth century B.C.E. and developed a fully democratic constitution modeled on that of Athens about 375 B.C.E.

Josephus calls the first Jews in Cyrenaica *katoikoi*, military settlers with land grants, a word not dissimilar to *etheloikeoi*, or Eshelokee.

For our purposes, the most fascinating aspect of ancient Cyrene that Appelbaum brings into relief is the unusual structure that served as a synagogue. It is apparently modeled after the amphitheater in the port of Apollonia, where the city-state's rites in honor of the sun-god Apollo/Ammon were carried out along with other solemn civic functions. The floor and pillars of the Jews' place of worship were plastered white, just as in the enactment of a ritual performed anew each year in the Cherokee national heptagon. The walls were colorfully painted—again like the Cherokee assembly hall and Pueblo Indian kiva. The architecture with its drum-like roof and seating arrangement about a hypostyle exactly duplicates the Cherokee layout.

But if the original language of the Keetoowah priests was Doric Greek as spoken in ancient Cyrene, what could be the historical link between Greeks, Jews, Libyans and Egyptians of that fabled cosmopolitan city-state and today's Cherokee of the Ozarks and Appalachians? How did they get from there to here? In the next chapter we suggest a motive and a way.

3 THE ESHELOKEE

Condemnation without investigation is the height of ignorance.
—Albert Einstein

WHEN I was invited to give an address at the annual conference of the Institute for the Study of American Cultures (ISAC) several years ago, I had no idea what to expect. Elephants in America! Jews in aboriginal New Mexico! Coxca in Mexico the hiding place of ancient Maya secrets! How Egyptians measured the equinox! Borneo the cradle of agriculture and navigation!

Although anthropological orthodoxy labels the work of diffusionists crackpot science—"Why do such lunatic ravings persist?" asks popular archeologist Brian Fagan in his book on human prehistory *The Great Journey: The Peopling of Ancient America*—diffusionist doctrine has been inching its way into the mainstream.

A case in point is a Greek admiral named Maui who, it is claimed, left inscriptions as far distant as New Guinea and Chile. According to Harvard biology professor Barry Fell, Maui was a third-century B.C.E. North African navigator in command of a large Libyan-Egyptian fleet. An extensive body of folklore survives throughout Polynesia concerning his exploits as a trickster and culture-bearer who "fished islands from the deep," somewhat like "many-wiled" Odysseus.

A New Zealander, Fell was keenly interested in elucidating the origins of the Maori, the ancient first settlers of his native land. He came upon cave drawings at Sosorra in western New Guinea, which he connected with an inscription in a cave near Santiago, Chile. After spending eight years "ransacking" Harvard's Widener Library, he was able to decipher the latter as an example of "standard Libyan . . . a dialect of Egyptian spoken by the brown-skinned fisher folk whom the Greeks called Mauri" (that is Moors, hence Maori).

There were hundreds of similar inscriptions scattered throughout the Pacific. Comparing the Santiago inscription and Sosorra drawings, which included paintings, astronomical and navigational diagrams and calculations in Greek and Egyptian, Fell reconstructed the events of an amazing feat of navigation in the ancient world. A Libyan fleet was dispatched between 235 and 225 B.C.E. under the auspices of Eratosthenes, director of the Library at Alexandria. Sponsored by the Egyptian pharaoh, its mission was to circumnavigate the world. It established what we now know as the international dateline. The admiral in charge was Maui, and the captain of one ship was Rata.

Berkeley geographer George Carter translates the Santiago inscription as follows:

> Southern limit of the coast reached by Maui. This region is the southern limit of the mountainous land the commander claims, by written proclamation, in this land exulting. To this southern limit he steered the flotilla of his ships. This land the navigator claims for the King of Egypt, for his Queen, and for their noble son.

The king, or pharaoh, referred to in this inscription is believed to be Ptolemy Euergetes III, called the Benefactor, whose wife was the Cyrenaic empress Berenice. He ruled until 221 B.C.E. Ptolemy III not only subjugated Libya (Cyrene) but his power is known to have extended as far eastward as India where King Asoka was his ally. (We will encounter King Asoka's name later on.) These facts date the landfall made by Maui's ships in South America to 230, as Ptolemy III began his reign in 246. Fell concludes that Rata, Maui and the three hundred or so other members of this expedition were the founding fathers of Polynesia.

If the Libyan presence in the Pacific during the third century B.C.E. consisted of an entire fleet, one separated from its homeland for several years, women were most likely aboard. The expedition was probably a colonizing effort.

The idea of a Ptolemaic colony in the Far East is borne out by the presence of Mediterranean mitochondrial DNA in Southeast Asia, Indonesia, New Guinea and Polynesia. Mitochondrial DNA is passed from a mother to her children unchanged over millennia, so it is a good tool for determining the founding mothers of populations. One study of New Guinea lineages finds a sizable degree of haplogroup (maternal lineage) H, a specifically European type. Its incidence does not seem likely to be due to modern admixture, as often claimed of such an anomaly, for such a conclusion would entail a nineteenth or twentieth-century European woman (say, an adventurous Victorian schoolteacher) marrying a native man.

Among the drawings in the New Guinea cave studied by Fell was a figure he identified as an "ancient Libyan instrument called the Tanawa, or 'Reckoner,' a mechanical calculator of the third century B.C. intended to aid the study of planetary motions by converting position angles from polar to ecliptic coordinates." Two subsequent experiments built models of the *tanawa* (from Greek τανάν 'outstretched, long') and proved it was used to determine longitude, an accomplishment not replicated until the eighteenth century.

The Cherokee may have perpetuated a folk memory of this mechanical marvel in the legend of the Tlanua, or Great Hawk, the name for which is almost exactly the same.

Despite mounting evidence, scholars summon all their ingenuity to dismiss ancient testimony that Greeks, Egyptians and other peoples of the Mediterranean could accomplish deep-sea voyages. An acknowledged expert on ancient seafaring, Lionel Casson in *The Ancient Mariners*, draws attention to three long-distance feats of navigation but manages for different reasons to belittle their importance. The first comes from Egypt. He recalls the "great state-operated maritime enterprise" to fetch myrrh and other unguents and incenses from a distant land called Punt, identified with lands on the Gulf of Aden or Indian Ocean coast of Somalia and Ethiopia. This was some 2,000 years before the modern era. The Pharaoh Mentuhotep III commissioned his minister Henu to cross the desert with 2,000 men, build a boat on Egypt's Red Sea port and sail south in a ship 180 feet long and 60 feet wide with a crew of 120 to establish a sea lane to the foreign source for precious ingredients used in Egypt's royal mummification process. Two months later, Henu returned home.

Casson goes on to explain, however, that the Punt trade lapsed for a long period in Egypt, only to be revived 500 years later. He thus implies that Henu's expedition was an isolated incident. In a perplexing argument, he assigns the "revival" of Egyptian seafaring to the next piece of evidence that happens to survive. It is one that can hardly be ignored. Its instigator was Queen Hatshepsut, the eighteenth-dynasty ruler who was one of only a handful of female pharaohs. (She wore the royal beard like Cleopatra.) Hatshepsut erected a monument displaying her fleet docking at Punt and leaving under full sail laden with goods that included "ebony, myrrh-resin, live myrrh trees . . . various other types of incense, ivory, gold, eye cosmetic, skins, 3,300 head of cattle, natives and their children . . . native spears, apes, monkeys, dogs, even 'a southern panther alive, captured for her majesty.'" So much for Egypt's feeble attempt to master the seas.

A third demonstration of seafaring took place, Casson continues, under Pharoah Necho in the seventh century B.C.E. After attempting to dig a canal between the Nile and the Red Sea, Necho commissioned the Phoenicians to undertake the circumnavigation of Africa from east to west to explore an alternative route to the southern seas (Indian Ocean). They were to come home into the Mediterranean through the Strait of Gibraltar.

Another feat of navigation discussed by Casson might better be called a massive colonization effort. It was a Phoenician scheme from about 500 B.C.E. to populate West Africa with 30,000 desert-dwelling Moors from the hinterland of Carthage, the new capital (in present-day Tunisia).

And so it goes. Does Herodotus write that the Phoenicians "were wont to visit . . . a nation beyond the pillars of Hercules (Gibraltar)" and trade trinkets with the natives for gold? A fable. Do Sumerian tables of the third millenium B.C.E. describe voyages "beyond the western sea" (the Atlantic) and establishment of colonies in a distant land? Surely, this could not be America, for that land had to wait 3,500 years to be discovered by a European. Never mind that Sumerian tablets with cuneiform writing were found in the nineteenth century in Lexington, Georgia, and a Sumerian tablet once in the possession of Chief Joseph of the Nez Perce tribe is displayed today in the West Point Military Museum. Did Barry Fell find correspondences between Ptolemaic Egyptian and more than 400 terms referring to mariners, navigation, astronomy, meteorology, justice and administration, medicine and economy in the Micmac and Abenaki languages of present-day New England? Coincidence.

The "Anthropological Monroe Doctrine" clearly states that there were no meaningful Old World influences in the New World before 1492 C.E.

Yet scholars have long been struck by cultural traits shared by Indonesians, Polynesians and Native American peoples. University of California, Davis, retired geography professor Stephen Jett draws attention to several similarities between Southeast Asians and Native Americans. The inhabitants of Borneo, for example, physiologically resemble Arawak Indians of the Caribbean. Natives in both regions use slash-and-burn agriculture, blowguns and head hunting trophies—customs found also among the Cherokee.

It is possible that the seacoast homeland of the Cherokee subject to floods and notable for its water monsters mentioned in so many accounts corresponds to the Sunda Shelf, a now-submerged part of Southeast Asia joined once with Indonesia and New Guinea. According to Oxford professor Stephen Oppenheim, this fertile and populous region was gradually inundated by rising sea levels beginning with the meltdown after the last Ice Age. Jett believes that migrations to escape flooding began about 3600 B.C.E. and lasted until as late as 300 B.C.E., the time of the first Polynesian voyages. Could this explain why the Vision of the Elohi speaks of an increasingly crowded land? Might it also account for the disappearance of the route taken across the ocean, one described as cut off, visible only in broken fragments on the ocean floor? The rising waters of the earth's new climate would certainly have produced a shifting and precarious new seashore. It makes sense that scattered islands sighted by the first voyagers in the Pacific were sometimes never found again since they could not turn back against prevailing currents and winds. It should be noted that the Libyan fleet never returned home.

For more pieces of the puzzle, let us turn now to Cherokee author William Eubanks. He was a member of the Keetoowah Society who wrote under the name Unenudi. Eubanks was a translator for the Cherokee Nation and indefatigable contributor to the Southern lecture circuit. Around 1900, he authored a tract titled *The Red Race, Originators of the Ancient Apollo Worship*. In it, he alludes to many of the same mysteries contained in the Vision of the Elohi, which, as we have seen, was published by him and attributed to Sakiyah Sanders.

Eubanks lends support to the idea of Greeks, Jews and Egyptians mingling together to form the Cherokee people when he writes:

> While the Cherokee is neither Greek, Hebrew, Egyptian, nor Hindoo, he has in his language many words purely Greek, Hebrew, Egyptian and Sanscrit, and while his ancient religious custom and rites bear a strong resemblance to the rites and

religious custom of the ancient Jewish religion, and his secret religion or mysteries is similar in many respect to the Egyptian, still there is strong evidence that he is neither Hebrew nor Egyptian.

He argues further that the Cherokee identity, or their true name, "has never been found out, and perhaps never will be," but it is a designation given to those "initiated as a tribe into the eastern mysteries . . . by a wise branch of the tribe known as those who spoke the language of Seg" (Asaga, Osaka).

What about the language called Seg? This is an enormously valuable clue. Seg is an Austronesian language of Indonesia, part of the very large language family known as Central-Eastern-Malayo Polynesian, with a western form called Thai-Seg and eastern form spoken in the Madang province of Papua New Guinea known as Sek, or Gedaged. The word points to the dispersals from Sundaland and initial sea voyages of the Melanesians and Polynesians, since it is the name of an important non-native clan in New Guinea.

According to Oppenheimer, the north coast of New Guinea acted as an important route for seaborne evacuation from the sinking landmass of Sundaland. In *Out of Eden*, his sequel to the book *Eden in the East*, he postulates that Island Indonesia teemed with life and was the source of new currents of agriculture and navigation. It was the true cradle of civilization, not India or Mesopotamia. Madang was the center for an eastward Polynesian diffusion that began about 500 B.C.E. Modern science associates these Austronesians and Malay people with the Lapita culture that spread a distinctive style of ceramics from Southeast Asia throughout Indonesia, Borneo, New Guinea and Melanesia as far west as Fiji and Samoa during the first three millennia B.C.E. Thus, an advanced, lighter skinned civilization from Sundaland mixed with Papuan-speaking (non-Seg) natives.

It is hard to resist the temptation to conclude that the latter, non-Seg natives correspond to the Cherokees' "black race of terrible invaders," who came in boats over the waters. These are presumably Austronesians and Melanesians who waged war against the Malaysian and Indonesian people from Sundaland. Recall that after repeated invasions there was no land to fight over since it all "sank into the ocean." To this day, there seems to be recognizable among Hawaiian Islanders as well as the Cherokees a certain Melanesian type.

There is evidence other than oral tradition that Polynesians joined the Cherokee. Aside from the Pacific Rim traits and characteristics like blowguns mentioned above, one of the seven Cherokee clans is called Anigilohi, the Twister People. This name should mean something like "people from Gilo" and can be taken as strictly Hawaiian. In Hawaiian, Hilo (there is no *g* in Hawaiian) means "braid, twisted." (Compare Greek *illa*, "rope"; *hilo*, "twist, wrap"; *hilex*, "twisting.") Gilolo was the land where the earliest ancestors of the Hawaiians came from, identified by later Spanish, Dutch and English navigators as the Moluccas in the Indonesian Archipelago.

The legend goes that Hawaii's capital city Hilo got its name from the natives' skill in twisting together plant fibers to make rope. The same root appears in hula, the dance ("twist"). Such a derivation explains why the Twister clan members "were once a proud people who strutted when they walked and twisted their shoulders in a haughty manner." The Anigilohi clan's cultural memory evidently reflects an ancient connection with the Polynesians who accompanied the Eshelokee—the People from Hilo. Such an identification may also explain why Twisters were considered by the other clans as extraneous foreigners, a group composed of prisoners of war, captives and refugees who had only a tenuous connection to the Cherokee. Chapter 4 presents several famous Twister Clan lines, often representing female lineage B, the classic Southeast Asian and Pacific Islander type.

Tagwadihi, a Cherokee medicine man photographed by James Mooney in the 1890s, not only physically resembles Native Hawaiians but also seems to bear a Hawaiian name, one that may be derived from Greek. We have seen how the word *dakwa* means whale or sea monster. Curiously, one of Maui's names is Talaga, very close to Tsalagi. Maui's father was Tangaroa or Tanoa (seemingly designating a Danaan or Greek). Tanoa was the father of all fair-haired children and came from a land called Atia.

Atia, which appears to be the same word as Attica, was the ancient Polynesian homeland to the West, full of high alabaster temples. One of them:

> . . . was very spacious, and was built as a meeting-place for gods and men; and here after death the spirits of the ancients foregathered with the gods. Here originated different kinds of sports, and games and feasts to the gods Rongo', Tane', Ruanuku, Tu', Tangaroa, and Tongaiti. Here were meeting-places for the great chiefs of those days . . . when appointing rulers, and devising measures for the good of the people. Here, too,

originated the wars that caused the people to enter and spread over the Pacific.

One could hardly invent a more fitting folk memory of Greek culture. Athens, the capital of Attica, was the envy of the world for its marble buildings dedicated to the gods of Olympus, its trade, games, amusements, learning, food, luxuries, art, philosophy, military prowess and democratic government. It is handed down that the ancestors of the Polynesians left this land when it was governed by the great king Tu-te-rangi-marama about 450 BCE, a date that corresponds exactly with Athens' golden age under Pericles. The Hawaiian word that epitomized this lost world is *karioi*, "leisure, ease," literally the same word as Greek "amusements." Christian missionaries fought to eradicate Polynesians' pursuit of *karioi*, often translating the beloved concept in English as "lewdness."

It seems that the Ani-Gotigewi, or Wild Potato Clan, just like the Twister Clan, exists only among the Cherokee. This clan seems to reflect the Eshelokee's travels in South America. Potatoes come from Peru and were not grown in North America until their introduction by Europeans. Could it be that the name of this clan in the singular, Gotigewa, pronounced approximately K'tigwa, is a corruption of Quechua, the original name of the Andean people we know today as the Incas?

What about the Paint Clan, Ani-Wodi? "Paint People" seems, without question, to be the customary term for Phoenicians, whose name for themselves was *Knai* "Canaanites." This appears to be rendered in Native America as Kanawa, the name of a tributary of the Ohio, and the Conoy Indians mentioned by Adair specifically as a Canaanite tribe. In the Old World, Phoinikoi, the Greek term, was used to designate people associated with the phoenix (a mythological bird that rose from its own ashes), the date palm and a reddish-blue or purple dye, all emblems of Punic civilization. Phoenician wealth was founded on Tyrian purple, a violet-purple dye derived from the *Murex* sea snail's shell. They stepped into the copper and tin trade of the Minoans after about 1200 BCE, moving their center of operations successively from Lebanon to Asia Minor to Carthage. Among the Cherokee, Paint Clan members were traditionally the doctors and hunters (*kanati*, from Greek *gennadi* "noblemen"), keepers of history (*tikano*, from Greek *tynchana* "events") and prophecy, and masters of protocol, diplomacy and ceremony. Peace chiefs and Ukus , "owls," or wise men in the Greek model, were often chosen from Paint Clan ranks.

It is significant that the Keetoowah culture-bearers in the Vision of the Elohi are called the "wise ones of heaven." The word for heaven used here is Galunlati, literally "The Up-Above Place." When Cherokee storytellers talk about the world before the present one it is either up above in a country called Galunlati or in the far West, sometimes called Elohiyi. It is said that gods and goddesses, people, animals, plants and every other type of being lived there until it became over-populated. This land still exists on the other side of the vault of heaven, which is hard as rock and impenetrable.

In antiquity, it was only the Egyptians, that is, Ptolemaic Greeks, as well as certain Asian peoples, along with the Cherokee and Hopi, who knew the world was round, not flat. It must have been a difficult concept to accept, even by highly educated and inquisitive minds of the day. Indeed, the theory slumbered in Europe until the Renaissance.

The Cherokee-Tuscarora medicine man Rolling Thunder had an astoundingly ecumenical worldview. Brian Wilkes, who studied under him, remembers he gave long talks about the pyramids, the Book of Exodus, Egyptians, Babylonians, Greeks, Jews and other ancient peoples. Finally, Wilkes said, "It sounds like our people were a lot like the Jews, Greeks and Egyptians." At this, Rolling Thunder looked sternly at him and snapped, "Our people were not *like* the Jews, Greeks and Egyptians; they *were* the Jews, Greeks and Egyptians."

Summing up, we may hypothesize that the Cherokee Nation of American Indians originated as remnants of Ptolemy III's expedition around 230 B.C.E. The mission was to circumnavigate the earth to test Eratosthenes' new concepts regarding its size and shape. Archeological evidence for this comes from cave drawings at Sosorra on McCluer Bay in Western New Guinea depicting, among other things, the *tanawa* navigational instrument used by Alexandrian Egyptian ships. Additional archeological clues are an etching of a Greek hoplite in Tennessee along with the form and function of the Cherokees' *cahtiyis*, or council house.

The Cherokees' tribal name Eshelokee originally meant Colonists.

Were the missing clans perhaps the five main divisions of the Hopi, the Bear Clan, Sun Clan, Reed Clan, Bow Clan and Flute Clan?

4 DNA

History does not repeat itself. The historians repeat one another.
—Max Beerbohm

FEW people know it but Elvis Presley claimed to be Jewish and Cherokee. A DNA test run on a rare specimen of his in 2004 bore this out. Both of Elvis' assertions were based on the ancestry of his mother, Gladys Love Smith. Growing up in Memphis, Elvis went to summer camp through the Jewish community center. When his mother died, he took care to have her grave marked with a Star of David (since removed). He studied Judaism increasingly in later years and to the end of his life wore a chai necklace, symbol of Jewish life. Published genealogies take Gladys' strict maternal line back to great-great grandmother Nancy Burdine, a professed Jewess born in Kentucky, whose mother was White Dove, a reputed fullblood. Through his mother's direct female line, Elvis was a Jewish Indian, an American Indian Jew.

Well, maybe not. Bracketing for the moment what makes one a Jew, we have to admit that American Indian identity is not so simple either. One factor weighing heavily in both claims, however, is DNA.

Paleo-American genetics is fraught with problems. According to a previous director of Tulane's Middle American Research Institute, the field is a notorious "battleground of the theorists," a controversial area "which has snared to their downfall not a few crackpots, mystics, 'linguistic acrobats,' racists and even 'famous institutions' . . .

[including] of course the anthropological profession itself." The DNA landscape is strewn with racist bombshells and political dynamite.

About twenty years ago, in a work as revered as it is unreadable, Italian-born geneticist Luca Luigi Cavalli-Sforza at Stanford University unveiled a tree of man based on an analysis of 120 markers from forty-two world populations. Looking solely at female lines, he posited two main limbs, African and non-African. The latter branched off into Europeans (Caucasians) and Northeast Asians (Siberians and Mongolians). Included in Northeast Asians were so-called Amerindians. Amerinds were closest in genetic distance to Northern Turkic, Chukchi and other Arctic peoples. They shared a number of genetic markers with their ancient neighbors, including a similar frequency of female lineages. These came to be labeled mitochondrial haplogroups A, B, C, and D.

Little did Cavalli-Sforza and his team expect to encounter any snags in their research, much less defunding by the U.S. Government and the United Nations, but this is exactly what happened. The genial professor received a letter from a Canadian human rights group called the Rural Advancement Foundation International. They demanded he stop his work immediately. They accused the Human Genome Diversity Project of biopiracy. The scientists were stealing DNA.

Ever since that slippery slope, geneticists have trodden warily around the issue of Native American demographics and genetics.

Theodore Schurr's team in 1990 had matched "Amerindian" changes in mitochondrial DNA over the last 40,000 years with those of Mongolians and Siberians. The lines were indelibly drawn. The scientific community laid down the law that the earliest Native Americans come from four primary maternal lineages. Only female haplogroups A, B, C and D are true Native American types. A fifth lineage, haplogroup X, was admitted, provisionally, in 1997.

Elvis's American Indian mitochondrial type is B. What account can we make of this haplogroup? Certain critics of the new axiom in American Indian genetics point out that B is not associated in high frequencies with Mongolian populations. Rather, it is Southeast Asian in origin—something borne out by the Elvis sample having also a rare Asian ethnic marker. B's center of diffusion is Taiwan and it is common, even dominant, among Polynesians, the Hopi, and Pueblo Indians like the Jemez.

Geneticists base their conclusions about ancient migrations on comparisons with population data of living peoples as reported in anthropological and forensic publications. But these are assumptions, pure and simple. Is it certain that populations in places like Mongolia and Alaska in the past—especially far distant past—were the same as they are today? Numerous genetic types become extinct in the course of time. Bottlenecks and genetic drift distort a population's structure and composition. Early migrants can be replaced through competition or changed by gene flow from later arrivals. Genotyping to determine a Y chromosome group from paternal pedigrees or the mitochondrial DNA passed to us by our mother, looks at but two lines out of thousands in one's heritage. The current state of genomics cannot test ancestry that crosses from a male to female or vice versa. It cannot isolate the genetic contribution passed to you, say, by your mother's father, or maternal grandfather. Most of our genetic history lies buried in non-sex-linked lines, the province of autosomal DNA.

Schurr's doctrine of the four ancient founding mothers of Native Americans was based entirely on small Pima, Maya, Ticuna, Mexican and South American Indian samples. A study by D. C. Wallace and colleagues inferred an Asian correlation from evidence taken solely from Arizona's tiny tribes of Pima and Papago Indians. This 1985 article was the source of untold mischief. Four female haplogroups were later "proved" to account for over 95 percent of all contemporary American Indian populations. Geneticists fell into lockstep to show that only a small number of founding mothers migrated from Asia into the New World. In 2004, despite a much shallower time-depth for calculating mutations, scientists decided that it had to be the same story for male founders. There was a single, recent entry of Native American Y chromosomes into the Americas.

The underlying logic goes like this: All our subjects tested out to be haplogroup A, B, C, D, E or X.

All our subjects were Indians because they were located on reservations.

Therefore, all Indians are haplogroup A, B, C, D, E or X.

It's as though we claimed, "All men are two-legged creatures; therefore since the skeleton we dug up has two legs, it is human." It might be a kangaroo.

About the time Rutgers professor Elizabeth Hirschman and I were concluding our study of Melungeon DNA, we decided to put together a small sample of Cherokee descendants who could trace their line back to the marriage of a Jewish merchant with the daughter of an Indian headman. Our object was to test the ethnicity of those

Cherokee who blended with Melungeons. Those enrolled for the project had to be directly descended from a Cherokee woman strictly through the female line.

To our knowledge, our studies were the first to qualify participants on the basis of their family histories. Invariably, these mention Indian ancestry in the female line, usually Cherokee. Native American chiefs cemented trade agreements with intermarriage of their daughters and other female kinswomen. Early explorer John Lawson wrote about this custom in 1709:

> The Indian Traders are those which travel and abide amongst the Indians for a long space of time; sometimes for a Year, two, or three. These Men have commonly their Indian Wives, whereby they soon learn the Indian Tongue, keep a Friendship with the Savages; and, besides the Satisfaction of a She-Bed-Fellow, they find these Indian Girls very serviceable to them, on Account of dressing their Victuals, and instructing 'em in the Affairs and Customs of the Country. Moreover, such a Man gets a great Trade with the Savages; for when a Person that lives amongst them, is reserv'd from the Conversation of their Women, 'tis impossible for him ever to accomplish his Designs amongst that People.

My forebear Isaac Cooper's grandfather was the pioneer William Cooper. This son of a plantation owner was born on the James River about 1725 and became the guide and scout for Daniel Boone when the latter was hired by the firm of Cohen and Isaacs to survey lands eventually forming Kentucky and Tennessee. Cooper planted a corn crop in 1775 on the left bank of Otter Creek above Clover Bottom near Boonsboro. He was then employed by Richard Henderson to assist Boone in clearing the Wilderness Road. He died in 1781 in an Indian attack after helping the Cumberland settlers continue the road to what became Nashville, Tennessee.

Although the Coopers came from England in the seventeenth century and settled on the James River, their more distant origins were clearly Portuguese and Jewish. They were descended from Marannos, who became British citizens in the period of the Glorious Revolution of William and Mary immediately following Jews' re-admittance into Britain. This path to Americanization is a staple feature of Cherokee genealogies.

Let us now turn to the female side of the project. Gayl Wilson traces her Wolf Clan line to Sarah Consene, a daughter of Young

Dragging Canoe. She is an enrolled member of the Cherokee Nation of Oklahoma. Her mitochondrial DNA haplogroup C proves to be one of the leading types among Cherokees. It is found sparsely in Mongolia and Siberia, and its frequency in North America is weighted toward the Northeast rather than Alaska and the Northwest, with a heavy incidence in the lower Appalachians. Wilson's particular type of C matches nine individuals with Hispanic surnames, including Juan B. Madrid (Two Hearts), a California schoolteacher, and 26 anonymous samples from Mexico, Peru, Puerto Rico, Spain and the U.S. This would appear to support the Mexican affinities of the Cherokee.

DNA that ended up being haplogroup B was contributed by a matrilineal descendant of Lucretia Parris, halfblood daughter of George Parris and granddaughter of early Cherokee Indian trader Richard Pearis, who died in the Bahamas, April 7, 1794. The Pearis or Parris family is the likely namesake of Parris Island in South Carolina. Their original name was perhaps Perez/Peres. They intermarried with the Dougherty and Cooper families.

U.S. federal Indian agent Benjamin Hawkins describes Cornelius Dougherty's residence near the town of Quanasee and calls him "an old Irish trader." He is said to have been 120 years old when he died in 1788. His original trading post was located at Seneca Old Town on the Keowee River, where William and Joseph Cooper were also situated since 1698. Cornelius' father Alexander was a Jacobite who fled to America after the Glorious Revolution. According to Rogers and Rogers' Cherokee history, it was Alexander who was probably the first white man to marry a Cherokee, in 1690. After 1719, Cornelius became a licensed trader out of Charleston, the British headquarters for the Indian trade, where brothers William and Joseph Cooper were commissioners, and married Ah-nee-wa-kee, a daughter of Chief Moytoy II, thus fulfilling the usual contract. She was of the Wild Potato Clan. Deerhead Cove beneath the brow of Fox Mountain in Dade County, Georgia and DeKalb County, Alabama, was named for her. The name of the mountain towering over Deerhead Cove honors Chief Black Fox, whose descendants on nearby Sand Mountain are multiply entwined with Doughertys.

Elvis' form of B matches Chickasaws, Choctaws and Creeks. Altogether, lineage B accounts for one-half or more of Cherokee DNA and roughly a quarter of all Southeastern Indians. The Maya and Mixté in Mexico are about one-quarter B and one-half A with smaller degrees of C, D and other. The Pima are about half B, half C, with a negligible amount of A. The Boruca in Central America are as high as three-quarters B.

When first described, haplogroup B was believed to be part of a second wave of American Indian colonization from Asia dating to 15,000-12,000 years ago. This migration supposedly followed an earlier and larger influx of A. The highest frequencies of B are found along the eastern edge of China in the islands of Taiwan (34%) and the Philippines (40%). Today, it is more likely to be seen as the trail of early humans following the beachcomber route up through Japan and down the American coast.

Elvis Presley was born and grew up in Tupelo, on the edge of Chickasaw country. But his maternal ancestor Nancy Burdine came from Kentucky in Cherokee territory. His remote female ancestor could have been either Chickasaw or Cherokee. The Chickasaw and Cherokee had a common border just west of the site of Nashville along the Natchez Trace. They often exchanged female marriage partners in peace treaties and intertribal relations.

Two Cherokee female lines show a connection with the white man who founded the Eastern Band of Cherokee Indians. Col. William Holland Thomas (1805-1893) occupies a special place in the history of the Eastern Band of Cherokee. He went to work at the age of twelve at the Walker trading post on Soco Creek and learned the Cherokee language as he bargained with the natives for ginseng and furs. Drowning Bear, chief of Quallatown, took a keen interest in him. When Drowning Bear learned that the boy had no father or brothers and sisters, he adopted him as a son. Will's best friend was a Cherokee boy who taught him the ancient customs, lore and religious rites.

In 1867 Thomas' health failed. The Civil War had ruined him. He eventually went into an insane asylum, where he died May 10, 1893. Without him, however, there would be no Eastern Band of the Cherokee Nation. Col. Will Thomas was the only white chief of an Indian tribe.

While he was an apprentice for the Walkers, young Will fell in love with Catherine Hyde, a descendant of Betsy Walker, a Cherokee woman from Soco (One-Town). A direct maternal line descendant of Betsy Walker, Kimberly Hill, provided a sample of her mitochondrial DNA. It proved to be a specific type within haplogroup J. The same haplotype came to light in fellow project participant Sharon Bedzyk, a descendant of Ann Hyde, Catherine's sister. A related haplotype was identified in a late-joining participant with ancestry traced to Myra Jarvis, a Melungeon woman born 1815 in Georgia.

Although Col. Will officially married Sarah Jane Burney Love late in life in 1857, he had several paramours. In addition to Catherine Hyde, one of them was the Polly after whom the Qualla Reservation was named. She bore him Demarius Angeline in 1827. Note that Demarius is a favorite name of Crypto-Jews. It is derived from Tamar, Hebrew for "date palm." Here again our project was fortunate. Thanks to the Indian grapevine, a direct female-line descendant of Demarius Angeline Sherrill, nee Thomas, responded to the call. "We were most surprised to learn our Angeline came from the X lineage," said James Riddle. He is literally the last of the line. Since he is male, Angeline's lineage would die out with him. It is an apt illustration of the fragility of haplogroups.

Haplogroup X was first detected in North America over a decade ago. It was added to Native American lineages A, B, C and D only reluctantly. Its discovery opened the door for more minor founding mothers at the same time that it created a strong incentive among die-hard believers in existing dogma to prove it was Siberian. What is different about haplogroup X is the suspicion it might be an ancient link between Europe and North America. Some view it as a founding lineage that directly crossed the Atlantic Ocean, perhaps with the elusive Red Paint Culture. The detection of X in our study represents the first report of it among the Cherokee. Previously, it was identified only in certain northern tribes.

We have seven instances of haplogroup X. In the case of Annie L. Garrett, born 1846 in Mississippi, descendant Betty Sue Satterfield vouches for there being a tradition in the family she was Cherokee.

Michelle Baugh of Hazel Green, Alabama, traces her Cherokee female line to Agnes Weldy, born about 1707. Descendants include enrolled members of the Eastern Band of Cherokee Indians.

Seyinus, a Cherokee woman born on or near the Qualla Boundary in North Carolina in 1862, is the source of a similar X lineage.

Another is the sample taken from Billy Sinor, the son of Gladys Lulu Sutton, born in Indian Territory in 1906. His mother's birth certificate lists her as "Cherokee Indian."

My own maternal line goes back to a Cherokee woman in northern Georgia or North Carolina who had children by a trader named Jordan. He can be identified as Enoch Jordan. Trader Jordan was born about 1768 in Scotland of ancestry from Russia or the Ukraine. His Cherokee wife, my 5th great-grandmother, proves to be haplogroup U2, but a form of it with no exact matches in any databases. Given origins in Russia or the Ukraine, and an intervening generation in Scotland, Trader Jordan himself was almost certainly Jewish. The Y chromosome type of his descendants belongs to male haplogroup J, a paternal lineage that contains the genetic signature of Old Testament priests. Here is evidently another case of a Jewish trader marrying a Cherokee woman. But how to explain the Cherokee wife's Old World haplogroup of U?

Haplogroup U is associated with Berbers and Egyptians as well as other early Mediterranean peoples. Professor Brian Sykes in *The Seven Daughters of Eve* places the *Ur*-mother Ursula he created for his bestseller in prehistoric Greece. The resemblance of members of my mother Bessie Cooper Yates' family, who claimed to be Cherokee through the female line, to a modern-day Cyrenaic woman in the Alinari photo archives seems striking and undeniable.

In our study, U covers 13 cases or 25% of the total, second in frequency only to haplogroup T. Who are these Mediterranean descendants among the Cherokee?

One is Mary M. Garrabrant-Brower. Her great-grandmother was Clarissa Green of the Cherokee Wolf Clan, born 1846. This Wolf Clan woman's grandfather was remembered as a Cherokee chief, as is consistent with the traditional nature of the Wolf Clan. Mary's mother Mary M. Lounsbury maintained the Cherokee language and rituals, even though the family relocated to the Northeast.

A Scottsdale, Arizona doctor in our study, another U, matches only one other person in the world, Marie Eastman, born 1901 in Indian Territory. His own descent is documented from Jane Rose, a member of the Eastern Cherokee Band. Her family is listed on the Baker Rolls, the final arbiter of enrollment established by the U.S. government.

My wife, Teresa Panther-Yates, proves to have mtDNA that can also be designated U, the most common "European" subgroup according to genetics journals. It has no exact matches anywhere; it is unique in the world. Teresa traces her maternal line back to Hancock County, Georgia. Her female ancestor died about 1838, at the time of the Trail of Tears. There is a tradition in her family that this line was Cherokee.

One participant who learned of her U lineage in the study says that her line goes back to Ann Dreaweah, a Cherokee woman married to a half blood Cherokee man.

Another instance of U has no close matches at all but appears to have a Cherokee form of it. He was adopted in Oklahoma and knows nothing of his mother's ancestry.

Gerald Potterf, another U, traces his mother's line to Lillie C. Wilson-Field, born in 1857, Catawba County, North Carolina. He believes she was probably Cherokee.

In all instances of U where there are Melungeon, Cherokee and Jewish connections in the genealogy, the most frequent clan mentioned is Paint Clan.

It was the T's, however, that blew the lid off Cherokee DNA studies. Haplogroup T emerges as the largest lineage, followed by U, X, J and H. Similar proportions of these haplogroups are noted in the populations of Egypt, Israel and other parts of the East Mediterranean.

Maternal lineage T arose in Mesopotamia approximately 10,000 to 12,000 years ago. It spread northward through the Caucasus and west from Anatolia into Europe. It shares a common source with haplogroup J in the parent haplogroup JT. Ancient people bearing haplogroup T and J are viewed by geneticists as some of the first farmers, introducing agriculture to Europe with the Neolithic Revolution. Europe's previous genetic substrate emphasized older haplogroups U and N. The T lineage includes about ten percent of modern Europeans. The closer one goes to its origin in the Fertile Crescent the more prevalent it is.

All T's in the Cherokee project are unmatched in Old World populations. They do, however, in some cases, match each other. Such kinship indicates we are looking at members of the same definite group, with the same set of clan mothers as their ancestors.

One T in the study fully matched four other people in the Mitosearch database, all born in the United States. One of these listed their ancestor as being Birdie Burns, born 1889 in Arkansas, the daughter of Alice Cook, a Cherokee.

Gail Lynn Dean is the wife of another participant. Both she and her husband claim Cherokee ancestries.

Linda Burckhalter is the great-great-granddaughter of Sully Firebush, the daughter of a Cherokee chief. Sully married Solomon Sutton, stowaway son of a London merchant, in what would seem to be a variation of "Jewish trader marries chief's daughter."

At twenty-seven percent, T types make up the leading anomalous haplogroup not corresponding to the types A, B, C, or D. Several of them evidently stem from the same Cherokee family or clan, although they have been scattered from their original home by historical circumstances. Such consistency in the findings reinforces the conclusion that this is an accurate cross-section of a population, not a random collection of DNA test subjects. No such mix could result from post-1492 European gene flow into the Cherokee Nation. To dismiss the evidence as admixture would entail assuming that there was a large influx of Middle Eastern-born women selectively marrying Cherokee men in historical times, something not even faintly suggested by the facts. Mitochondrial DNA can only come from mothers; it cannot be brought into the country by men.

If not from Siberia, Mongolia or Asia, where do our anomalous, non-Amerindian-appearing lineages come from? The comparative incidence of haplogroup T in the Cherokee mirrors the percentage for Egypt, one of the only countries where T attains a major showing among the other types. In Egypt, T is three times the frequency it is in Europe. Haplogroup U in our sample is about the same as the Middle East in general. Its frequency is similar to that of Turkey and Greece.

Far and away, however, the most explosive evidence revolves around haplogroup X, the third largest haplogroup. The only other place on earth where X is found at such a prodigious frequency is in the Druze, a people who have dwelt for thousands of years in the Hills of Galilee in northern Israel and Lebanon. The work of Liran I. Shlush in 2009 proves that the Druze, because of the high concentration as well as diversity of haplotypes, is the worldwide source and center of diffusion for X.

In conclusion, there may be a reason why Elvis claimed to be Jewish and Native American and loved Hawaii.

5 THE MISSISSIPIAN-ERA CHEROKEES

Anyone undertaking to set himself up as judge in the field of truth and knowledge is sure to be shipwrecked by the laughter of the gods.
—Albert Einstein

PRE-COLUMBIAN Indians not only developed advanced societies with ingenuous technologies and beautiful works of art but also shaped the land and left their mark on the very geography of North and South America. It was only the ravages of European disease and attendant decimation of Indian populations that created in the minds of the invaders a lasting impression of savagery and inconsequence—one perpetuated by scientific notions down to our day.

It's as if an "American Middle Ages" never existed, as Barry Fell noted when he wrote that "fragments of pottery have been made the basis of our interpretation of history."

With the benefit of Constantine Rafinesque's outline of American Indian history, we can now take a closer look at some of the native nations inhabiting that chasm of the past, including the Real People or Cherokees. Rafinesque writes in his *History of the Ancient Indians*:

> Something like a chronological order can be now introduced. The records of the Mexicans, the traditions of many Oghuzian nations [Uighur Turkic, i.e., the Algonquians' Wallam Olum], and the annals of the Europeans, afford sufficient materials for a complete history; but I must be very brief.

Nearly two thousand years ago [200 B.C.E.], great revolutions happened in the north of Asia; the Oghuzian empire was severed, and a swarm of barbarous nations emigrating from Tatary [Mongolia] and Siberia, spread desolation from Europe to America. In Europe they nearly destroyed the powerful Roman empire, and in North America they subverted many civilized states.

Several of those Oghuzian nations, driven by necessity or their foes to the north-east corner of Asia, came in sight of America, and crossing Berhing [sic] Strait on the ice, at various times, they reached North America. Two of them, the Lenap [Delaware] and Menguy [Iroquoian tribes], seeking milder climates, spread themselves towards the south; while another, the Karitit [Eskimo], which came after them, spread on the sea shores from Alaska to Greenland, and some others settled on the north-west coast of America [Haida, Tlingit et al.].

These events correspond to the first period of the Algonquian people's history as presented in the restored Wallam Olum of David McCutcheon. There we read of a multitude "ten thousand strong" crossing "the frozen sea at low tide in the narrows of the icy ocean." Twenty-four chiefs' reigns pass as they spread and settle in Turtle Island (North America), migrate to the Snake (Enemy) River (present day Washington and Oregon, where there are still at least two Algonquian-speaking tribes, the Yurok and Wiyots of California, that were apparently left behind) and make their way across the interior to emerge in the Mississippi River valley, defeat the Talegans and cohabitate with them on the Wabash River in Indiana. McCutcheon calculates this span of time as one of 500 years on the basis of 13-2/3 years per chief. If we take Rafinesque's starting point for the invasion to be around 200 B.C.E, this brings us to around 300 C.E. for the Algonquian army's progression to the eastern shore of the Mississippi. Here the Algonquian armies conquer the Natchez (Iztacans) and Talegans (Atlans mixed with Iztacans). McCormick's chronology compares well with Rafinesque's:

A settlement was made east of the mountains, and the great Lenapian nation became thus divided into many distant tribes, independent of each other; but connected by a similarity of language, religion, manners, and acknowledged origin.

A similar division took place in the Menguys, and the independent nations sprung from them, were the Hurons or Wyandots near lake Huron, the Eries or Erigas on Lake Erie in Ohio, the Tuscororas in Kentucky, the Senekas [Seneca], Mohawks [Iroquois], Cayugas, Oneidas on the St. Lawrence, &c. That portion of the nation which remained west of the Mississippi [e.g. Blackfoot and Cheyenne, two Algonquian-speaking Plains tribes], became mixt [sic] with some Otomian [Sioux] tribes, and formed the great Darcota [Dakota] nation, since divided into many tribes, such as the Sioux, Assiniboils [Assiniboine], Tinton [Teton Sioux], Yanctons [Yankton Sioux], &c.

Here occurs one of the first explicit mentions of the Cherokee. They are presented as a third force in a power play between the Iroquois (Menguy) and Lenni Lenape, the core Algonquian nation, showing they had probably broken with their allies the Iroquois for the second time. A Lenape legend tells how the Iroquois stirred up a war against the Cherokee by killing a Cherokee child and leaving a Lenape war club on the scene as evidence. This tale may relate to those distant days.

That the Iroquois, like the Cherokee, once lived on the other side of the Mississippi is apparent from several sources. One of these, a Tihanama Indian story, relates that the Iroquois encountered the Lakota Indians for the first time on the grassy prairies across the Mississippi. "Who are you," the Iroquois asked them. The Lakota replied, "We are hunters of the buffalo. Who are you?" "We are hunters of men," said the Iroquois and challenged the Lakota warriors to a contest on the spot. "You are not men," said the Iroquois, after winning the fight, "but women." They split the Lakota warriors' noses (the mark of an adulterous woman) and sent them on their way. "Tell your people to send men the next time," they said.

The Cherokee (Eshelokee), then, crossed the Mississippi about the same time as the Algonquians and Iroquois, around 300 C.E. All these tribes take up residence in the area along the Ohio vacated by the Talegans, Natchez (Iztacans) and remaining eastern Siouan tribes (Otomi).

In McCutcheon's version of the Wallam Olum, we read that before crossing the Mississippi, somewhere along the south bank of the Missouri, the Algonquians encounter a foreign tribe they call the

Stonies under a chief named Strong Stone. The latter is depicted with an angular headdress of five horns unlike any other in the Red Record. "Strong stone" is an apt description of metal. The prominent headdress could represent a Greek hoplite's stallion crest. This style distinguished the Eshelokee warrior and seems later to have been imitated by certain local Plains tribes like the Pawnee and Poncas. Known as a porcupine roach, it is a prized part of Indian regalia. Hardly any leading man or fancy dancer at a powwow today would be without one.

The millennium between 300 and 1300 C.E. witnesses the breaking off of the Iroquois to migrate onward to their historical locations concentrated in Upper New York State, along with the formation of the Shawnee dominions southward and the Lenape advance eastward. Sometime during this era, corresponding approximately to the Mississippian Period of archeologists, the Cherokee break for the second time with the Iroquois. The Cherokee migrate to the southern Appalachian Mountains in East Tennessee, where they wrest a new homeland for themselves from the assorted Muscogean, Yuchi and Natchez tribes already inhabiting the area.

As we have seen, evidence for ancient Greeks in America is sparse, but compelling. Traces of the Greeks may explain the migrations of the Eshelokee through Mexico and are borne out by Keetoowah traditions. It is clear that after the Cherokee's exodus with the Huichols from Toltec Mexico they lived for several centuries in the Oklahoma-Arkansas- Missouri region, remembered in legend as The Land of Sorrows. Finds of a bronze Athenian medallion along with two examples of a coin from the Athenian colony of Thurium on the Red River in Oklahoma suggest one tarrying place where they stayed. Here they must have clashed with the Iroquois and adopted the Iroquoian language as a peace concession, for when the Algonquian army arrives around 300 C.E., they join it as the Stonies (Armored Men). The three nations cross the Mississippi, defeat the Natchez and Talegans and live together in a state fluctuating between friendly and hostile for a thousand years until the Shawnee begin to build up their hegemony over all tribes.

The Cherokees, Iroquois, and Algonquians, including the Shawnee, did not build mounds; only the Iztacan Indians from Mexico raised these monuments. Principal among the Iztacan or Uto-Aztecan Indians were the Natchez, who, as reported by Rafinesque, were forced out of the Ohio Valley by the incoming Algonquians and Iroquois (called by him Oghuzians). By the time of recorded history under the Europeans, the domains of the Natchez recede within the surroundings of the city named for them on the lower Mississippi. Only the Natchez Trace and its continuation the Avery remained to show that their empire once stretched into Kentucky. It is documented fact that they built their last mound in 1712 shortly before being brutally slaughtered and dispersed by the French.

In the late 1700s, the Indian agent Benjamin Hawkins took several Cherokee leaders to see the Etowah mounds situated just north of present-day Atlanta. They told him these were not the monuments of those who now held the land, the Creek, but of Indians who came before the Creek. We may identify these as Iztacan tribes like the Natchez.

The Atlantic shores of America were not unknown to the ancient Greeks, nor were they unvisited by the Minoans, Egyptians and Phoenicians before them. In Strabo's *Geography* of about 25 BCE, America is called Epeiros Occidentalis, the Western Continent. Writing in the first century CE, Plutarch describes the northern sailing route and records that the Western Continent lay 5,000 *stades* beyond Greenland. He also mentions a southern route beginning in the Canary Islands followed of old by Phoenicians. This information seems to be based on the earlier writer Diodorus Siculus (1st cent. BCE). Plutarch writes also that Greeks founded a colony among the indigenous peoples across the Atlantic. A Greek tetradrachm found in Cass County, Illinois, dating to between 175 and 164 BCE seems to indicate that Hellenistic-era Greeks navigated up the Mississippi at that time. There is an abundance of other signs for Greeks in the Americas.

As we have seen, archeologists are just beginning to develop a chronology for the Mississippian Period, conventionally set in the years 1200-1600. Occasionally, however, a random window opens up on these blank centuries. The Rocky Creek Stone is just such a testimony. It is, I propose, a record of the Cherokee conquest of their new territories in the Cumberland and separation from the Shawnee. The 19x15 inch engraved limestone tablet was exhumed in 1870 in a Mississippian Period mound on Rocky Creek near Castalian Springs, Sumner County, Tennessee. It is now in the possession of the Tennessee Historical Society and is periodically on exhibit at the Tennessee State Museum in Nashville. Engravings were published and partially elucidated in 1890 by Gates P. Thruston in his *Antiquities of Tennessee.*

I will go further than Thruston and say that the Rocky Creek tablet evidently commemorates a peace treaty concluding a war between the newly arrived Cherokee and the Shawnee, whose stronghold by then was in Middle Tennessee.

The tablet shows us a Cherokee with a war club, far left, identified by his distinctive topknot, four scarification marks across his face, the traditional sign of a chief, and sun symbols on his skirt. (The Cherokee were so proud of their topknots that a silver cylinder to hold them in place was one of the most popular trade items bartered to them by English traders out of Charleston in the 1600s and 1700s.) He battles a Shawnee warrior distinguished by Mohawk hairdo, feathers, spear and large square shield with "sky-serpent" design. The Cherokee side evidently carries the day. The Shawnee sue for peace. The two tribes smoke the peace calumet in a longhouse of the Shawnee hung with checkered wampum belts (bottom center).

The two chiefs are reprised on the right of the tablet, dressed now in ceremonial attire, the Cherokee wearing a horsehair crested helmet and carrying the spear and shield of a Greek hoplite, the Shawnee clasping hands in a wedding ceremony with his Cherokee bride bearing wampum belts as a pledge of peace. She has her hair in a bun, the sign of maidenhood, and wears a Middle Eastern-style plaid kilt displaying a large six-pointed star on her breast. The groom has brought the requisite blanket and bag of meat to exchange. Thanks to the union of the two, the Cherokee and Shawnee people are now on the path of peace (symbolized by the horizontal lines beneath them) rather than warpath.

The Cherokee chief has a gorget about his neck in the shape of a crescent moon, below it a sun, and there are sun signs also on his skirt and shield: A similar configuration of quarter moon and sun was depicted on the posts of the Cherokee council house, the *cahtiyis*. The early Cherokee like the ancient Greeks, Egyptians and Libyans were sun-worshippers, calling themselves "a great nation known as the Eshelokee of the half-sphere temple of light" (*Vision of Eloh'*). The Shawnee man, on the other hand, is identified by a double serpent design on his shield. Above him and going through his head is a longhouse or village with a serpent and other clan symbols over it, encoding, doubtless, its name – perhaps Turtle Town? These pictograms resemble those of the Wallam Olum, while the Cherokee writing system, on the other hand, appears to be ogam, a Mediterranean script.

The six-pointed star adorning the Cherokee woman seems to me clearly to be a star of David, emblem of Judaism. In my experience, no other type of star like it can be adduced from Indians of this time period. She wears a skirt of woven cloth and bracelets, both exotic touches. Of the skirt's pattern, it may be pointed out that Thruston found numerous instances in the same area of what he calls the "familiar Greek key or classic fret pattern." Citing his predecessor Conant, he also notes that human figures from nearby excavations are shown "clad in flowing garments gathered by a belt around the waist and reaching to the knees"—a perfect picture of the tunics and chitons of ancient Greeks. Cave murals discovered in 1883 by the archeologist Priest in Ohio tell the same story: Their location now unknown, they depicted Indians with Greco-Roman toga-like costumes. Further, an Egyptian-style mummy with Greek writing on the wrappings was untombed on the Cumberland River near Carthage, Tennessee, in 1815—not far from Castalian Springs. As described by the antiquarian Haywood, it was a young woman with blond hair wearing a silver clasp on her wrist.

The old-time Cherokee unashamedly glorified their bodies. Their athletic orientation can be explained by the original Spartan and Dorian Greek cast of their society. David Sansone in his study of athletics in the ancient world notes a correlation between Cherokees and Greeks in this respect without suggesting any real historical link. He points to "numerous and striking parallels between the practice of the Greeks in connection with athletes and that of the Indian ball players," although he remarks that there is "no question of direct contact" between the two. Ascribing the coincidences to a common origin in the magical practices of prehistoric hunter societies, Sansone explores repeated correspondences between the Greek rituals surrounding the Olympic Games and Cherokee athletes' preparation for ball play, a form of lacrosse. They extend to "prohibitions against specific foods," a taboo against intercourse with women for a period of one month before and seven days following an event, disqualification if the athlete's wife is pregnant, bathing before and after in a nearby river, and a fire ritual.

Both Cherokee and Greek athletes scraped their skin before the pre-game bath. The Cherokee scored it "with an implement designed to produce parallel superficial gashes" just before a ballgame. Greek athletes used a toothed sickle, replaced later by a smooth-edged strigil, to scrape and scarify their muscles. Cherokee men submitted to having a comb with teeth of turkey spurs or some other sharp object (*canuga*, "scratcher"; compare Greek *kanon*) dragged across their bodies before plunging seven times in a stream. The scoring of skin was supposed to strengthen athletes and help them win. The sickle or strigil, "with which we may compare the Cherokee turkey-bone comb," says Sansone, opened the surface of the skin to allow the purifying waters of the bath to soak in and any weakness or illness to escape: "The function of the strigil was analogous to . . . that of the turkey-bone instrument used in the Cherokee scratching ordeal. The pain thus caused was considered an act of sacrifice."

Archeologists have noted the distribution of so-called chunkey stones from 600 C.E. in a southward pattern. Their spread exactly fits the time and direction of the Cherokees' travels before they settled in the southern Appalachians. The prized heirlooms (from the root *tlan-*, meaning "swoop down, fall") were housed in Indian temples and clan houses, and they seem to be the same as the Greek *diskos* ("thing to pitch"). The discus throw was one of the five sporting events along with the javelin in the Greek pentathlon, the main contest of the Olympic Games. Indian chunkeys come in many sizes but are usually round, flat, polished stones about twelve inches in diameter. They were used in a contest between two men on a sandy playing field. Bets were wagered by the spectators. One player hurled the stone so that it rolled as far as possible in a direct line while the other ran forward a few yards to a line and threw a javelin at the traveling chunkey. The first player then threw his javelin. Whichever came closest to the chunkey when it came to rest determined the winner. Chunkey stones were often of venerable antiquity and were owned by the religious hierarchy of the town, not individuals. Like the Greek discobolus depicted in a familiar ancient Greek statue by Myron, Cherokee athletes competed in the nude, or at least bare but for breechclout. Curiously, it was a tradition recorded by the first pioneers in Abingdon, Virginia, that the Indians used to have intertribal sporting events at Blackmore's Fort every four years; the custom was discontinued shortly after the English arrived.

Finally, let us consider the figure of Stoneclad, or Stonecoat. This culture hero must come from the Cherokee's Stony Tribe past. He is a fierce warlock "responsible for bestowing on the Cherokees specific medicinal formulas and knowledge, hunting songs, the crystals [*ulungstata*, cf. Greek *ouluntata* "judged healthy"] used for divining, and the red clay used for face and body painting." His "whole body is covered with a skin of solid rock." He is a flesh-eating warrior with a long sharp instrument he uses for killing people, and he is called an *askili* or *tsasgili/tchaskili*, "witch," a name for one of the types of Cherokee spiritual practitioners which can also mean owl. I suggest *tchaskili* or *tchaskiri* in the Lower Cherokee dialect, with its telltale foreign *ts-* sound, comes from Greek. It appears to be a corruption of the Greek word for 'Thracian'.

When Stoneclad dies he is given a funeral pyre. He sings forth all of his magical charms and storied knowledge for everyone to hear and bequeaths to the seven clans a firm foundation for the Cherokee Nation. Ever afterward it is taboo for any Cherokee to add to the stories and songs of old (*tikano*, cf. Greek *tynchano* "to come to pass").

According to musicologists, the Cherokee greatly favor "anhemitonic scales." One of these five or six note scales is built into every Southeastern Indian flute made today. It can be simulated by playing all the black notes on a piano keyboard. One hears it in the harmonies of many country music songs, an industry that originated in the Cherokee's former homeland of Tennessee. The "harsh" but harmonic Dorian mode of country music pickers and the Southeastern flute underlies much of American Indian music, particularly that of the Hopi, Zuni, Pima and Cherokee. To get an idea how it sounds, think of the song "What Shall We Do with a Drunken Sailor," the Beatles' "Eleanor Rigby," or the Doors' "Light My Fire." Most of the Doors' songs, in fact, are in the Dorian mode. Cherokee stomp dance songs have melodies in the slow sections that are anhemitonic. The closest analogs in Native America appear to be Hopi, Zuni and Pima music.

Cherokee music is also noteworthy in featuring water drums and leg rattles, instruments with a deep history in Egypt.

6 THE CROWN OF TANASI

O could their ancient Incas rise again
How would they take up Israel's taunting strain!
—William Cowper

BRITISH colonial officials recognized the usefulness of having natives visit England as soon as possible. There they might be overawed with the mother country's wealth and intimidated by its formidable military might. Between visiting the Tower of London and going to plays and rat catching shows, such delegations had their official portraits painted by court artists. As recounted in the book *Indians Abroad,* they then returned home with news about the teeming numbers of Englishmen and hopeless odds involved in fighting King George. They also acquired a taste for English goods. My ancestor Attakullakulla ordered a pipe organ to be delivered to his home in the Tennessee wilderness so his wife might learn to play it. He had been intrigued by the one he saw in St. Paul's Cathedral.

One of the records of these visits by Indians to Europe is a large oil painting titled "An Audience Given by the Trustees of Georgia to a Delegation of Creek Indians (1734-35)." It is now owned by the Winterthur Museum in Delaware but it used to hang in the Trustees' offices in London. In it, the sponsors of the new colony of Georgia are assembled at their London headquarters receiving a visiting party of Indians usually identified as Creek. The painting is the work of William Verelst, a Dutch master who painted for the court. The nominal occasion is the 1734 state visit of Tomochichi (died October 5,

1739). Tomochichi was the Yamacraw Indian who befriended the colony's founder, General James Edward Oglethorpe. Tomochichi opened many doors for the English settlers in Savannah. This painting was displayed in the Whitehall offices of the Trustees as long as they continued in existence. To this day, reproductions can be found in museums and offices across the state of Georgia and beyond. Upon dissolution of the Trustees in 1752 and conversion of Georgia to a royal colony the original passed to Anthony Ashley Cooper, fourth Earl of Shaftesbury. It remained in the Cooper family until acquired by the industrialist Henry Francis du Pont in the 1930s. In 1926, the ninth earl presented to the state of Georgia a copy painted by Edmund Dyer in 1826.

Despite the original painting's fame not much is known about it. Art critics assume it was based on preliminary studies, either live sessions or renditions, and that the work was completed over a period of several years following the Georgia Indians' visit to London in June to October, 1734. Of the painter, Edgar P. Richardson writes, "William Verelst belonged to one of those transplanted families of artists whom the English think of as Dutch and the Dutch think of as English and who are, in consequence, ignored by both." Art reference books contain scant mention of him. Another Verelst, Jan, probably a cousin, is better known. He painted official full-length portraits of the five Iroquois Confederacy chiefs who visited Queen Anne in 1710.

If the artist is mysterious, his subjects, at least the Indian ones, are even more so. All the Englishmen are identified. These include the President of the Trustees, Viscount Percival, Earl of Egmont, the Earl of Shaftesbury and Oglethorpe. But of the Indians, only Tomochichi is named. He appears prominently in the center of the scene handing a devotional book to an Indian boy. The Indians fill the right half of the canvas, in a formal diptych opposite the white men, with an interpreter identified by some as John Musgrove interceding between them and the British. On the frame of a later copy of the painting the Indian boy is identified as Toonahowi, Tomochichi's nephew. The sole female figure is Senauki, his wife. A portrait or study by Verelst of Tomochichi and his nephew confirms these identities.

The other five Indians, including the conspicuous young man in the foreground with a Mohawk hairstyle, have never been identified. In most reproductions they are simply labeled "Indians," "Creek Indians," or "Yamacraw Indians." I will demonstrate they are not Creek, but Cherokee.

Our first clue is the small-framed Indian holding a fan in the foreground. This is fairly obviously Attakullakulla, who visited England with a party of Cherokees in 1730, four years before the Creek mission. Investigation of the diplomacy of the delegations of 1730 and 1734 supports this identification. French Algonquian Indians were prominent in the affairs of the Cherokees in this period.

The Spanish, Portuguese, Dutch, English, and French had radically different ceremonies of possession by which they legitimized their claims in the New World. The English method was normally to make surveys and treaties and mark their possessions with houses, gardens and fences. Often a twig or piece of turf was presented from the old owners, the Indians, to the new ones. Colonies were thus imagined as plantations, plantings of English agrarian society in a foreign setting.

France employed a different approach. If the English model was grounded in a national love of gardens and *le confort anglais*, the French rite of possession rested, according to historian Patricia Seed, on a flair for drama. It was staged along the lines of the *joyeuse entrée* featuring a French monarch or lord entering a free city. Key elements were elaborate costumes, dancing and music. Amid festivities, the people gave their open consent to receive the visitor in hospitality and friendship. A French explorer describes his expedition as "conquest not by arms, but by the cross, not by force, but by love which has sweetly led them to donate themselves and their country to the king of France." As a consequence, the French enjoyed better relations with the Indians.

Certain elements in the Audience painting reflect a French concept of diplomacy. This should not surprise us at a time when Parisian court life and opera set the tone for other countries. The English, it must be remembered, were at this time trying to woo Indians away from the French. And so the overall scene is one of stately entry, festivity and joy. Tomochichi is painted with a definite, if artificial smile, reaching out the hand of friendship.

So what actual models did Verelst use for the five remaining Indians? Why were these not identified? There are several possible answers to these questions: 1) the English did not know the Indians' names, 2) their names have been lost through an accident of history, 3) the five Indians were not thought important or 3) they are not whom we suppose them to be.

The last alternative is our best explanation. The Indians are not who we might think they are. The Trustees had good reason to omit the names of Tomochichi's attendants and lump them together with no tribal identity if they were actually from a previous delegation. Significantly, the Creek Indians returned to Savannah before their portraits could be done, except for Tomochichi and his family. No Indians were available in London as live models during the years Verelst worked on the painting from 1734 to 1735. The representations of Creek chiefs Hillispilli, Apakowtski, Stimalchi, Sintouchi, and Hinguithi are feigned portraits. Attaching their names would have been a transparent fiction.

Let us consider next what the true identity of these Georgia Indians might be by looking at a previous attempt at British treatymaking. In 1730, a scapegrace Scots laird by the name of Alexander Cummings traveled to the Overhill Towns of the Cherokee and captured what he later called the Crown of Tanasi. Originally intending to bring back the "king," Moytoy, he persuaded instead seven countrymen, mostly younger Cherokees, to meet George II in London. His main contacts in Cherokee country were the brothers William and Joseph Cooper, traders based at Keowee in South Carolina. We have encountered the Cooper name before. Evidently William and Joseph Cooper belong to the same Marrano family as Robert Cooper, the London merchant whose DNA we analyzed before. The Cummings adventure resulted in an unofficial alliance between the Cherokee and English, though the Board of Commissioners ended up giving little credit to him. Later, the treaty was repudiated by the Cherokee chiefs. An outraged war party looted and burned the Coopers' trading post.

The famous Crown of Tanasi which Cummings had his Cherokee captives lay at the feet of the English sovereign was tossed aside in a royal closet at Hampton Court and never seen again.

The Scottish baronet from Aberdeen responsible for this fiasco is described by modern-day writers with words like "bizarre," "madcap" and "eccentric." In and out of debtor's prison, he died in ignominious circumstances. One of his more audacious schemes was the establishment of a stock company that would settle 300,000 "honest and industrious" European Jews among the Cherokee Indians. This white elephant may have been inspired by John Law's Mississippi Bubble. Cummings also claimed to be the "deliverer of the Jews." That he himself was a Jew seems more than likely from all the circumstances of his life and career. "He was called by his mother, a few days before her death, both Jacob and Israel."

If we ask how Cummings even *knew* of the existence of 300,000 Jews, a fairly accurate estimate of Ashkenazi Jews in Eastern Europe at the time, some surprising facts emerge. Like many Aberdeen burghers, he spent the first part of his career as a merchant and soldier in Russia and Lithuania. He may have retained connections with eastern Jewry, for "wild as his projects were, some of the most learned Jews seem to have given him several patient hearings on the subject." One can infer that Sir Alexander was an Aberdeen Crypto-Jew. The family name comes from the Flemish nobleman Comyns, a knight who accompanied William the Conqueror to England and boasted of being directly descended from Charlemagne. The Cummings clan's association with Gordons, Sutherlands and Setons supports Jewish roots.

While the seven Cherokee were in London, their movements were followed closely in the press. A popular engraving was made of them in the clothes that had been presented to them by the king. This etching is said to have been done by Isaac Basire "after a painting by Markham," now evidently lost. Shown in St. James's Garden, they are identified as Onanconoa, Skalilosken Ketagustah, Kollannah, Oukah Ulah, Tathtowe, Clogoittah and Ukwaneequa. The last mentioned, Uk-uk-u-ne-ka (White Owl), is small of stature, slender of frame and boyish-looking. He wears his hair in a Mohawk, a sign he is a Northerly, or Algonquian. As suspected at the outset of this inquiry, he can be none other than Attakullakulla (Ata'gul'kalu, "leaning wood"), supreme peace chief of the Cherokee 1760-1775. The engraving (and painting) captures him at about the age of 20. Since there is no mention of a youth among the visiting Creek and Yamacraw Indians other than the boy Tooanahawi, this must be Attakullakulla. The 1730 etching shows him carrying the eagle feather wand that the Cherokees presented to King George. In the 1734 painting he has the same feather wand. The Quaker naturalist Bartram described him as "a man of remarkably small stature, slender and of a delicate frame, the only instance I saw in the [Cherokee] Nation; but he is a man of superior abilities." In later life, Attakullakulla often mentioned his trip to England and offered to go back and see "the Great King George."

So who are the other Cherokees in the painting? Tathtowe (Tistoe, a ceremonial title meaning "smoke maker") is the tall figure with dangling side locks. In the 1734 grouping, he is evidently the headman of Keowee remembered as the fifth to join Cummings' party in 1730. The Cherokee title Tistoe distinguished an official responsible for smudging or producing the sacrificial smoke in the assembly house. Today it refers to Santa Claus, bringer of firecrackers during holidays. The word probably comes from Greek *typho* "to raise smoke."

The short figure on the extreme right in the 1734 painting is Clogoittah ("gun carrier," another title). He was from Tenase (Tanasi), the home of the Crown, fourth to join Cummings' party. The older man behind Tomochichi in the 1734 painting, second from the left in the 1730 etching and labeled Skalilosken (Speaker) Ketagustah (Second in Command) are the same persons. The Cherokee title *skalilosken*, which cannot be analyzed into Cherokee elements, seems to come from Greek *kerux*, "herald." In both instances, it is a title borne by the man responsible for summoning an assembly, delivering "talks" and making diplomatic contact with the enemy. Our Kittagusta, in reality, was probably the son of French Huguenot trader John Beamer and a Cherokee woman named Quatsis/Quatie ("Patsy/Patty"). Appropriately, Kittagusta the Speaker was chosen by the 1730 delegation to make a ceremonial speech in response to the treaty drafted by the British.

The muscular war chief in the foreground of the 1734 painting is the same figure as the one in the background of the 1730 etching. He is Collanah (The Raven) of Settico, brother of the same Quatsis/Quatie. That this is Collanah of Settico, not the Creek/Yuchi war chief Umphichi, follows from the facts as we have established them, namely, that Umphichi died before the audience with the Trustees took place. The brother of the mother, or maternal uncle, was considered the head of the household according to Cherokee custom. Hence Collanah stands behind the Speaker Kittagusta and Mankiller, his sister's children in the 1730 etching.

The remaining two Cherokees from the 1730 delegation do not appear in the 1734 painting. They are: 1) Outacite (Mankiller) Skiagusta (Great Warrior), headman of Tassetchee, the second to join Cummings' party after Attakullakulla, and brother of Skalilosken Kittagusta, called Ukah Ulah (Principal Chief to Be) by the English, and 2) Ounakannowie (White Deer), second from the right next to Attakullakulla, a last minute addition to the Cummings party from the Upper Towns. Thus, three of the seven are members of Quatie's family, situated at the time in the Cherokee town of Tassetchee. One might speculate that Verelst omitted the chiefly figure of Outacite since the role of a headman in the 1734 scene was filled by Tomochichi.

Summing up, Verelst's graphically realized details show there was a lost painting or study upon which his portraits were based. Markham's painting (and the engraving inspired by it) depicts the Cherokees in English clothes, but the Trustees painting has them in native dress. Perhaps an intermediary picture from 1730 was discarded after the Cherokees revoked the treaty, but used out of convenience as a mold for the Trustees painting in 1734.

Two members of the 1730 delegation, Kittagusta the Speaker and Collanah the Raven of Settico, previously of Tassetchee, are evidently mixed, not full bloods. Collanah exhibits a muscular build atypical of American Indians, more like black slaves or Europeans. Cherokee historian Brent Cox says Collanah, brother of Quatie, married Nancy, who was "one half white." It was unusual at that time for an Indian male to marry a white or part-white woman: The inference is perhaps that he also bore some non-Indian genes. There could have been African ancestry in his parents' makeup. The names Quatie (Patty) and Nancy (Nanheyi), moreover, are not originally Cherokee names.

John Beamer (Beamor, French Benamour, Sephardic surname Benamor) was a French Huguenot of an Iberian Jewish family fleeing from the Spanish Inquisition. His father came to the Carolina colony soon after the foundation of Charles Town. Beamer met Quatie in 1699; he was thus one of the first white men, along with Alexander Dougherty and Joseph Cooper, to intermarry with the Cherokee. She was his Indian wife; he had a series of white wives back in the settlements, one of them the daughter of the governor. On the frontier he received the name Beaver, Cherokee *Amadohiyi*, English Moytoy. Cox regards this as a clerical error but why should we not take it at face value? One meaning of the word is "beaver," another is "mariner."

We know that John Beamer's grandson, Thomas Beamer, was called a Mustee, proof of some degree of African blood. Derived from Mestizo, this term is confined to admixtures of the Indian and Negro races. In the Beamer-Moytoy family, then, we can trace –genealogically and pictorially—a tri-racial mixture later known as Melungeon, the white constituent in which is Sephardic Jewish.

By the year 1730, there was a significant degree of admixture among the Cherokee, including French, English, Portuguese, Spanish, Moroccan, Scottish, African and Jewish strains. This admixture appears to be concentrated in the ruling families of the largest Overhill Towns, Tellico, Echota and Settico, located primarily in what is now Monroe County, Tennessee. English, Scottish and French merchants out of Charlestown, typically Sephardic Jews, were the first to intermarry with the Cherokee.

It has often been maintained that the office of principal chief was not introduced among the Cherokees and other southeastern tribes until the British created it, wishing to have a single authority to deal with on matters of trade. English policy was to appoint headmen to sign treaties for all towns in their "nation." As R. S. Cotterill, for instance, says of the 1721 treaty at Congaree, the British "created, on [Gov. Francis] Nicholson's suggestion, the new office of principal chief, elevating thereto a chief whom the Carolina writers have effectively disguised as Wrosetasatow [a form of Outacite, Mankiller, from the Lower Town of Estatoe]." The historian Charles Hudson agrees that principal chiefs did not come into fashion until the mid-eighteenth century, when a breed of Indians who might be termed "Fort Indians" gathered around the trading posts built on the southeastern frontier. Moytoy, Old Hop, the "non-entity" Amascossite, Attakullakulla and Oconostota thus serve as treaty chiefs for the Cherokee. In the same way, Tomochichi and the "Emperor" Brim function as puppets manipulated by the English in Georgia. Conchak Emike (Chief Skunk-Hole) fulfills the same role among the Choctaws until the French have him killed.

Such a picture of tribal government may not be completely accurate. The principal actors in the Cherokee Nation at this time were Jews. The Stuart monarchs had long favored Portuguese and Scottish Sephardim because they knew that Jews harbored an abiding hatred of the Spanish. If captured, Marannos and New Christians would be burned at the stake as heretics. They knew it. For this reason, Savannah Jews of Sephardic background fled to nearby Charleston during the brief War of Jenkin's Ear when it seemed the Spanish might invade Georgia. Only Ashkenazi Jews like the Sheftalls remained behind. How much of Jewish participation in Cherokee politics was opportunistic and how much was borne out of the traders' recognition of genetic and religious ties cannot be known, but the official titles used by the Cherokee delegation of 1730 confirm the story of the Eshelokee. Most of them are Greek and military in inspiration, from Moytoy (Admiral) to Skalilosken (herald) and Kolanu (*karanos*).

The true origin of the Uku or Peace Chief explains the significance of the Crown of Tanasi, for the Uku traditionally wore an otter headdress. After nearly two thousand years, and in their own way, the Cherokee retained many of the customs of the original Eshelokee. No ordinary colonists these. They appear to have been selected for intellectual standing and superior knowledge. One leader was a philosopher-king. Another was called the Admiral.

7 THE MOTHER GODDESS IN AMERICA

Stars we cease to believe in grow pale.
—Heinrich Heine

NANCY Ward is one of only a handful of women we know about in the history of Indian nations to be given the title Beloved. In Cherokee, she was called the Ghigau, the Beloved, Red, Honorable, or War Woman. She received this honor in 1755 attending her husband Kingfisher in a war party against the Creeks in Upper Georgia. She performed tasks customary for women, such as cooking, carrying water and gathering firewood. But when Kingfisher was slain before her eyes, she took up his bloody tomahawk and helped rout the entire Creek army. She tied the captives, cattle and slaves and drove them home. In Chota, the Cherokee seat of government, she was elevated to the highest position a woman could hold. As the Ghigau, she decided whether or not a captive taken in war would be killed or adopted into the tribe.

Nancy came from the Moytoy family examined previously. Her mother was Tame Doe and her father Sir Francis Ward, a Scottish laird at the nearby British outpost of Fort Loudon. A close relative of hers was Nionee, wife of Attakullakulla and mother of Dragging Canoe, the last great Cherokee general. Another of her names was Tsistuna-gis-ke, "Rose." This seems to be what Muslim Indians called her, perhaps the Creeks, for the surname Ward in Arabic means "rose." One of her relatives, John Ward, was a Tunisian pirate who converted to Islam and became known in Muslim annals as Wardiyya ("of the rose"). A Jacobean play lambasted Ward, whose flagship was manned by an Anglo-Turkish crew of four hundred pirates. This Barbary connection, like the Deer Clan of her grandfather, the Algonquian Indian White Owl Raven, seems to relate to the presence of Arab and Muslim culture in the eastern United States at the time, how old or extensive it is difficult to say.

Years after Nancy's death her memory was still alive. Someone carved a life-sized statue out of native granite and placed it over a grave in the Arnwine Cemetery overlooking the Clinch River, near Liberty Hill in Grainger County, Tennessee. In the 1970s, the unusual memorial was stolen by grave-robbers who spirited it away in a brown Chevy never to be seen again by the locals. Fortunately, D. Ray Smith, a descendant, had photographed it.

In Cherokee tradition, heroes and heroines are often associated with, and typified by, a mascot or namesake animal they capture, save or domesticate. In some cases, a woman would suckle a fawn or cub. It is no longer remembered how Nancy's mother Tame Deer received her name but it may have been for such a reason as this. The name of the powerful Uktena-slaying magician Oconusti of Cherokee legends means Groundhog Mother and was given to him because he showed a tender heart to an orphaned baby groundhog. The question is: What animal does Nancy Ward hold in her arms and foster, and why?

The statue shows Nancy displaying a coat of arms with her name on it along with the words "Watauga 1776." The Watauga Country was a bold experiment in government established by the followers of Daniel Boone in their attempt to carve out a free state in what is now East Tennessee. Elizabeth Hirschman has shown that there were religious as well as political motives behind the establishment of Watauga and has suggested that many of its leaders were Crypto-Jews. It is Nancy's dealings with the Wataugans that make her career inscrutable. Over and over, she commits daring betrayals of her people, sends secret warnings to the enemy and engages in risky reversals of war council policy.

One tale from many will illustrate Nancy Ward's habitual knack for incensing the rest of the Cherokee by perversely favoring the Wataugans. When the American Revolution broke out, the tribe leaned strongly toward the British cause under their agent John Stuart, a Scotsman, who had been formally adopted into the Wolf Clan by the Moytoy family. Cherokee warriors in the Overhill Towns could not wait to join their Lower Town and Middle Town brothers in striking back at the white settlements. Impetuously, they mounted a skirmish on the eve of the planned attack and captured outside Bean Station Lydia Bean, William's wife, along with thirteen-year-old Samuel Moore. They intercepted Mrs. Bean as she was making her way from her home on Boones Creek to Sycamore Shoals. The warriors marched the white female and boy to the Overhill Towns and strapped them to a stake. At this juncture, Nancy Ward called a stop to the proceedings. She told them that they could use Mrs. Bean's knowledge. In this decision, the Beloved Woman was exercising her right to spare a condemned captive's life. But she went much further. She took the injured Mrs. Bean into her own home and nursed her back to health. Samuel Moore was freed.

Mrs. Bean, like most colonial women, wove her own cloth. At the time, the Cherokee were wearing a combination of traditional animal skin clothing and loomed cloth purchased from traders. Cherokee people had rough-woven hemp clothing, but it was not as comfortable as that made from linen, cotton or wool. Mrs. Bean taught the Ghigau how to set up a loom, spin yarn and weave cloth. This skill would make the Cherokee people less dependent on traders, but it also Europeanized the Cherokee in ways little fathomed at the time. Women came to be expected to do the weaving and house chores. Men took over duties in the cornfields and became settled farmers. The females became dedicated housewives.

The design of the Nancy Ward statue focuses on her protection of the white settlers, and this connection may also explain the young cub or kit in her arms. Plainly not a lamb, or bear cub, or panther's kitten, it is rather a black fox (*Martes pennati*). This animal was evidently chosen to allegorize the new leadership promoted by the Beloved Woman's actions.

One of Nancy Ward's other names is Nunnehi, which may be translated One Who Goes Where She Pleases, a reference to a fairylike folk of the same name. These figures in Cherokee folklore are also called Anetsageta, a word related to *anetsa* "games" and clue to their deep ancestry. The likely Doric Greek root is *neika* "game, play." Anetsageta would of old have been understood to mean something like "The Playful or Mischievous Ones." The various terms are conventionally rendered as Little People in English. Literally, though, the term Nunnehi means "living, going anywhere." It can also be taken as "people of the paths." It is this designation that recalls their distant origins, for these Immortal Ones of Cherokee legend are descendants, anthropologically speaking, of the Fates of Greek and Roman religion. In Hebrew folk belief, they are the *hadas*. In Celtic mythology they are usually known as fairies. But all are one and the same.

Like their antecedents in the Old World, the Nunnehi are generally heard but not seen. They are oddly perverse and do things backwards. They live in caves and abandoned mounds but also have a council house under the water of lakes and rivers. Sometimes a beautiful Nunnehi woman will steal a young man away from the dance and take him home to their subterranean dwelling, exactly as in the story of Thomas Rhymer and the Fairy Queen. They can also help lost travelers. If they take a pot or other utensil from the household they always pay the owner back for what they "borrow."

Modern-day Cherokee beliefs based on "actual reports of encounters" with the Little People are recorded in a book published in Cherokee, North Carolina in 1998.

> When the Little People visit Cherokee homes, the kitchen seems to be their favorite room of the house. They like bright things such as silverware, pots and pans or shiny appliances. According to many stories one can often hear these items being moved around and afterward find them out of place. They seem to come to play with these things or to look at themselves in the mirror surfaces. They don't usually take anything unless they are hungry.

> Since the Little People seem to especially enjoy it, the Cherokee women often leave cornbread for them on the kitchen table. Frequently, the ladies report, the cornbread is gone the next day with crumbs left on the table or trailing across the room to the kitchen door.

If we compare these accounts of Indians' Little People with a study by authority Katharine Briggs, we see that the Cherokee versions incorporate, story by story, all the stock motifs of European fairy tales: brownies or house spirits making noises, poltergeists, pixies and pouks misleading travelers, will o' wisps, the supernatural passage of time in fairyland, shape shifting, the power of bestowing good or ill luck, caves as an entrance to fairyland, changelings (one of the earliest traditions), stealing food (or at least sucking nourishment out of milk and bread—a memory of the Homeric offering to ghosts), levitation (but no wings, a Victorian and very late invention), bargaining and exchanging items of trade, trooping and inflicting illness or helping with miracle cures.

In the Middle Ages the Fata of Greco-Roman belief systems recur as the Fées of France, *hadas* of Iberia (a word derived from *fata*) and fays, or fairies, of the British Isles. As before, "they visited the house where a child was born, with gifts of good and evil fortune" and in "sophisticated fairy tales . . . they became fairy godmothers." Among the Jews of Spain, a widespread custom was to celebrate all night with a *veula* or vigil prior to a boy-child's circumcision in order to bring good luck and ward off evil from the baby. This ceremony is the origin of the practice of throwing a gold or silver coin into a male infant's first bath to bring riches, a custom still practiced by Melungeons. The *hadas*, as Jews call the festivity, is a vestige of the Roman celebration of the Fata. The Sephardim of Spain also practiced a *fadamiento* for female children, which took place on the occasion of their naming dinner. As Judaic scholar David Gitlitz describes the celebration, the extended family would wait seven days before feasting and then shower the baby and its mother with presents. According to Cherokee tradition, if one wishes to join the Nunnehi, one must fast for seven days before going to them.

Nancy Ward was not actually called "She Who Walks with the Little People" but Nunnehi, one of the fairy folk themselves. With this name, she recalls the familiar figure of the Fairy Bride or Fairy Queen. She is a changeling as well as change agent. Her erratic actions in sometimes aiding the Wataugans against the war party's better judgment and sometimes shrilly denouncing them gave her a certain aura of the anomalous and other-worldly. She acquired a powerful influence. Nearly every Cherokee alive can find a connection to Nancy Ward in their family tree. It has been estimated that her known descendants number over 6,000. She left a dual legacy as the peaceful Beloved Woman and fierce War Woman, an ambiguity masterfully captured in the design of her funerary monument. She was not only a tribal mother. She became one of the immortals.

Up to this point in our narrative, we have heard more of men than women. Besides Nancy Moytoy and Nancy Ward, are there other well-known Cherokee women? Is there a significant cult of the female among the Cherokee? James Adair claimed the Cherokee had "petticoat government." Along with the Iroquois and Hopi, Cherokee are often mentioned as a people who placed a special emphasis on matriarchy. But the word matriarchy gives perhaps a false impression. As Riane Eisler, reminds us in her book *The Chalice and the Blade*, "matriarchy" means "rule by mothers," whereas early societies before the institution of domination patriarchies seem to have been egalitarian. "To describe the real alternative to a system based on the ranking of half of humanity over the other, I propose the new term *gylany*," she writes, going on to explain that her coinage comes from the Greek words for man and woman, linked neutrally. Once in our sights, gylany seems in abundant evidence as a worldwide societal phenomenon before about 3000 BCE, when it, together with the Mother Goddess religion underpinning it, yields universally to the blood-and-thunder sky-gods of warrior societies. Did anything like gylany ever exist in the ancient Cherokee world? Was there a time when, as archeologist Marija Gimbutas, archeo-psychologist Erich Neumann, classical scholar Jane Harrison and a host of other writers suggest, both Cherokee men and women worshipped a Mother Goddess as the bringer of life and supreme deity?

We can start with the recent past and have a look at the sacred formulas of the Cherokees collected by James Mooney around 1900. We note that in love charms, the lover prays to the spider or the moon. The spider has several aspects, in the north, east, south and west, and is in fact the heavenly spider invoked in several cures as the most powerful healer. Oddly, the moon is conceived of as a woman, whereas the Cherokee usually regard the moon as masculine. "The prayer is addressed to Age'yaguga, a formulistic name for the moon... The shamans can not explain the meaning of the term, which plainly contains the word *age'ya*, 'woman' ... The ordinary name is *nunda*, or more fully, *nunda sunnayehi*, 'the sun living in the night.'" In one prayer, the ruler of life is called the Terrible Woman "most beautiful" and described as residing with the Elohi of legend in the Far West. "There in Elahiyi you are at rest, O White Woman. No one is ever lonely when with you."

A recent study of Southeastern Indian religious objects includes a contribution on the enigmatic and arresting humpbacked Old Woman effigy vessels that have attracted the attention of archeologists and antiquarians since the earliest white settlement of Tennessee in the 1790s. One typical of the genre was excavated in the Campbell Site in the 1960s; it shows a red and white painted, covered ceramic bottle in the shape of a corpulent woman with her mouth open, squatting, with no arms. A figurine in the same tradition comes from Noel Cemetery in Sumner County, Tennessee, five miles south of Nashville off Franklin Turnpike on Browns Creek. "Among the numerous human effigies of the hooded-bottle form throughout the Southeast—and especially in the three most productive regions of northeastern Arkansas, southeastern Missouri, and central Tennessee," observe Carol Diaz-Granados and James R. Duncan, "humpbacked figures are extremely common." These experts present hooded female effigy bottles uncovered in pristine condition from the Averbuch site in Davidson County in the late 1970s, of a type they call "without doubt the single most important subject in the pottery of the Middle Cumberland Culture." But their interest is especially aroused by the Woman in the Patterned Shawl variant of the Old Woman, a humpbacked, kneeling female figure with prominent breasts and bun hairdo folding her hands in her lap and wearing a boldly patterned dark cloaklike garment and fancifully trimmed knee-length woven skirt.

I am going to make a case for a single interpretation. I propose that the Old Woman is the same as the Mother Goddess. The humpback that baffles Americanists like Diaz-Granados and Duncan has been amply documented in the work of Marija Gimbutas and others. Like the exaggerated hips and enormous rump of the Stone Age Venus of Willendorf, the humpback symbolizes the mysteries of the female body, a vessel that swells with pregnancy and the milk of nourishment. Images of the fertility goddess or earth mother abound in the literature wherever we look, provided we look. Often a pregnant woman holding belly with hands with breasts emphasized and masked face is shown. The mystical and abstract transformational aspect of the goddess (Apuleius' Juno or Hecate) can be traced back into the Middle Stone Age. Innumerable masked figurines in the publications of Gimbutas show M signs, V-shaped necklaces and butterflies symbolizing the waters of life, milk, nourishment and regeneration. Many of these exhibit the Bird Goddess' open mouth and closed eye motif, found on both sides of the Atlantic. Tri-lines represent the triple aspect of the goddess (birth, marriage, death), and the double swirl stands for the deity's forces of transformation—woman's powers of bringing to birth and taking away into death. Both in America and the Middle East and Europe, the Goddess is Mistress of Game and Livestock, with the deer, panther, fox and bear her magical companions. Universally, she is Giver of the Crafts of spinning, weaving, metallurgy and music.

By way of concluding, let us return to the name invoked to call out to the moon goddess in Cherokee prayers. As we saw, Age'yaguga could only be partially explained by white anthropologists. They recognized the first element in it as Cherokee for "woman" but could not determine what the second part meant. Well, *guga* is Cherokee for "bottle." When the Cherokee first came to Indian Territory, they dubbed Bartlesville Gugu-i because the English place-name sounded to them like Bottlesville. Accordingly, the name of the supreme Cherokee deity must be Bottle Woman.

8 YOM KIPPUR WITH THE CHEROKEE

*On Rosh Hashanah it is written, on Yom Kippur it is sealed; how
many will pass on, how many shall come to be? Who shall live and who
shall die? Who shall live to see ripe age and who shall perish?*
—Jewish Yom Kippur Service

BY all accounts, the Cherokee did not observe the sort of animistic-shamanistic spirituality practiced by many of their neighbors. They were scornful of the "barbaric" rites of the sweat lodge, sun dance and coming-of-age rituals of the Siouan tribes, as reported by eighteenth-century explorer John Lawson. Mexico, they said, was inhabited by six tribes of cannibals. They had hardly any better opinion of the cruel sutees and grisly boneyards of the Natchez.

In a series of articles about the religion of American Indians appearing in 1862, Cherokee newspaperman John Rollin Ridge wrote that they, in general, rejected the preaching of the missionaries. As evidence, he reprinted the famous speech of Red Jacket. When questioned whether Christians worshiped the true God, the Seneca chief replied that he would wait and see if their religion made them behave any the better. Ridge held that the Cherokee took their religion from the ancient Greeks, Persians, Jews and Chaldeans. They were superior in this respect, as in many others, to "the Athabascan, the Algonquin, the Iroquois, the Decotah, the Apalachian, the Chicorean, and the Natchez."

Important sources for Cherokee religion are the papers of Presbyterian missionary Daniel S. Butrick (1798-1851) and pamphleteer John Howard Payne housed in the Newberry Library in Chicago. John Payne was an indefatigable activist on behalf of Indian rights who is often remembered only as author of "Home Sweet Home." Of a Long Island Jewish family, he became an adopted Cherokee tribe member. In later years, he served as American consul to Tunis.

The Payne Papers include accounts of the seven Cherokee festivals and other aspects of the history, culture and religion of the tribe. One salient feature in them is the weight given to stories of Wasi (Cherokee for Moses). Wasi is more important than Jesus for the Cherokee, notes Butrick. Most commentators see this as evidence that the Cherokee learned Bible stories from traders. Given what we now know about the Eshelokee, however, these stories possibly predate Jewish traders of the eighteenth century. Might they not, like the name Elohi, actually be vestiges of the Cherokees' Mediterranean origins?

If Jews were not on board from the beginning, they certainly had arrived in Cherokee country by Roman times. In the 1960s, Minna Arenowich was working in her flowerbed on Cedar Street in Columbus, Georgia, when she dug up a bronze Roman coin. It bore the image of Antoninus Pius (emperor 135-161 C.E.). Archeologists often dismiss such finds because they do not come to light in the course of an official excavation. Who is to say someone did not plant a Roman coin in Minna Arenowich's garden? Perhaps it was a souvenir brought over by early settlers?

The same dismissal, however, cannot be accorded to the Bat Creek Stone. This small stone engraved with Hebrew was exhumed in a mound containing the skeletons of an East Tennessee chief and eight retainers by the Smithsonian Institution in 1889. Bat Creek is a tributary of the Little Tennessee River in Cherokee country about thirty miles southwest of Knoxville.

The stone's reference to the Jewish hero Simeon Bar Kokhba seems genuine—a connection first made by Cyrus Gordon. Discovered directly beneath the skull of the dignitary whose burial it marks, it proclaims, "Comet for the Jews," a slogan of the revolt against Rome in 132-135 C.E. This final bid for nationalistic sovereignty in ancient times was led by Simeon Bar Kokhba, whose name means "Son of the Star." It is a short leap to wonder whether the elite personage of the tomb was either a relative or leader of survivors from Bar Kokhba's revolt.

Who interred these warriors? From the elaborateness of the entombment it must have been their own people. An enclave of compatriots? That the burial is not an isolated instance of Jewish settlement in the region seems clear from coin finds:

> Coins struck during Bar Kokhba's regime have been extracted in Kentucky – Louisville 1932, Clay City 1952, Hopkinsville 1967—and in southeastern Missouri from the St. Francis, a tributary of the Mississippi, 1922. . . They read in Hebrew *Simeon* lower right around to lower left on the obverse and "Year Two [133 A.D.] of the Deliverance of Israel" on the reverse.

All these pieces of the puzzle converge on Melungeon territory. A similar lead comes from the Ramey family of Tennessee—an unrecognizable type of writing that turned up in the family's North Carolina attic in the 1990s. The script was written by Thomas Ramey, a circuit preacher and spy, in coded messages during the Civil War in Tennessee. It stymied most experts until identified as a variety of a Demotic Coptic "cipher" script similar to ones long used in Alexandria in Egypt. The substantial horde of writings continues to be kept under wraps by the family out of fear their contents might get them into trouble.

The Rameys, like many others mentioned in this book, were evidently Marranos. The origin and meaning of this term is disputed, but it appears to have first gained currency in the mid-fifteenth-century anti-Jewish riots in Toledo and Cordova. Its heyday for usage was the sixteenth century, when Jews escaping Spain and Portugal to other Catholic countries were denounced as "judaizers" by the Inquisition and Spanish crown. According to an entry in the *Jewish Encyclopaedia*,

> The wealthy Marranos, who engaged extensively in commerce, industries, and agriculture, intermarried with families of the old nobility; impoverished counts and marquises unhesitatingly wedded wealthy Jewesses; and it also happened that counts or nobles of the blood royal became infatuated with handsome Jewish girls. Beginning with the second generation, the Neo-Christians usually intermarried with women of their own sect. They became very influential through their wealth and intelligence, and were called to important positions at the palace, in government circles, and in the Cortes; they practised medicine and law and taught at the

universities; while their children frequently achieved high ecclesiastical honors.

None of the usual explanations given for the origin of the term Marrano seems compelling, least of all the suggestion that the word is derived from Spanish *marrano* "wild pig." Certainly over-ingenious is Hebrew scholar B. Netanyahu's claim that it comes from "a haplologic contraction of the Hebrew *mumar-anus* (which caused the omission of the first syllable), effecting the transformation: mumaranus, maranus, marano, marrano." If we look it up in Latin dictionaries before the modern period we find nothing about pigs, only a definition in civil jurisprudence of *maranus* as "privileged Jewish administrator who feigns to be Christian."

Evidently, the Egyptian title *maran* (meaning something like Sir) may have been carried by the conquering Arabs to Spain and retained for use in their civil administration. It then gave birth to Spanish *marrano* and survived in common Jewish surnames Moran, Morene and Moren as well as in Marianne, a favored name for girls in Jewish, Cherokee and Melungeon families. One doubts that the Moran and Moreno families of France, Scotland and Italy are embarrassed by the thought that their name might mean "pig" in Spanish.

Whatever the antiquity of the Jewish strain in Cherokee religion, it is clearly pre-rabbinical and pre-Diaspora. It is reminiscent of a state religion like that practiced by the Jews in their homeland before the destruction of Jerusalem by the Romans in 70 C.E. James Adair reaches a similar conclusion:

> . . . the Indian system is derived from the moral, ceremonial, and judicial laws of the Hebrews, though now but a faint copy of the divine original.— Their religious rites, martial customs, dress, music, dances, and domestic forms of life, seem clearly to evince also, that they came to America in early times, before sects had sprung up among the Jews, which was soon after their prophets ceased, and before arts and sciences had arrived to any perfection; otherwise, it is likely they would have retained some knowledge of them, at least where they first settled . . . .

These words indicate he thought that the Cherokee Jews belonged to the time of the First Temple (ca. 1000 B.C.E.) or even before. Yet on the basis of a detailed comparison of religious rites it is really not necessary to place their origins earlier than the inauguration of the

Second Temple in Jerusalem in 516 B.C.E. and reorganization of Jewish religion under Ezra beginning in 458 B.C.E. Jewish customs could have been planted in the Appalachians as late as the first and second centuries C.E., to judge from the Bat Creek Stone. The Cherokees' celebration of the New Year seems to reflect Jewish practices in the style and fashion of the Second Temple.

The Cherokee reckon the start of the New Year on the first new moon of the first month of autumn, Tishri in the Hebrew calendar. For the Brooklyn Jew as well as Oklahoma Cherokee, this falls sometime between September 5 and October 5. Ever since the Second Temple this date inaugurates the Days of Awe, or Repentance, and it ushers in the most holiday-intensive period of the year, a season focused on purification and renewal. According to first-century C.E. Jewish philosopher Philo of Alexandria, an old name for Rosh Hashanah (Head of the Year) is the Day of the Sacred Moon. In Cherokee, this holiday is called the Great New Moon Festival. In both cultures, the New Year is followed after exactly eight days by a second holy day considered the most important of the entire yearly cycle. Yom Kippur (Day of Atonement) in the Jewish faith and the solemn Propitiation Festival in Cherokee religion bear the same approximate name. Both follow the New Year by a week.

The similarities do not end there. The Jewish conception of the New Year is a time of reflection, of coming to terms with the past year, of purification, resolutions and predictions. Jews of old believed that the Almighty One maintained books in which he wrote the names of those who will live and those who will die in the coming year. Hence the greeting of temple congregants to each other, "May you be inscribed and sealed for a good year." Hence also the passage in the Yom Kippur service, "What was written on Rosh Hashanah is sealed on Yom Kippur."

During Rosh Hashanah, devout Jews eat tongue to symbolize the *head* of the year. So also on the Cherokee New Year hunters present the tongue of the first-killed buck deer to the Uku. This he uses for a sacrifice while the priests conduct divinatory exercises with crystals to determine which of the people are to die before the first new moon of the following spring.

In Jewish observance the afternoon of Rosh Hashanah is occupied by a second ceremony associated with the New Year, Tashlikh ("casting away"). This involves going to water and casting away the sins of the previous year. The Cherokee engage in a remarkable enactment of the same rite:

> Two hours before sunset, the Uku's principal assistant ordered everyone to go to the water . . . . As they waded in, the men went upstream and the women and children went downstream. Everyone quickly faced east [the direction of Jerusalem] and plunged entirely under the water . . . . Some people followed the custom of wearing old clothing, and while in the water, they disrobed and let the old clothing float away. This carried all their impurities away with it.

Between the first and second holy day, Cherokees fast on the fourth day, an apparent echo of the Jewish Fast of Gedaliah on Tishri 3. In Cherokee practice their Day of Cementation is preceded by a 24-hour period of fasting. It has a special liturgy with a unique melody, just like the Kol Nidre ("all vows") of Yom Kippur. Adair notes the similarity of the music in both cases. This is also the time, Adair says, when the ancient hymn *Ye ho waah* was sung. Of this hymn, informants observed that it:

> . . . could only be sung by selected persons on "occasions of the greatest solemnity." The hymn played a special role in the exciting Cementation Festival [Day of Reconciliation, i.e. Yom Kippur]. . . . The words . . . were described as being part of "the old language."

The Cherokee Propitiation Festival seems to reflect a third holiday of the Jewish high holy days, Sukkot, the Festival of the Tabernacles. Portions of this very old holiday seem to be incorporated in the harvest celebration called the Exalting, or Bounding Bush, Festival. Like Jews today with their myrtle boughs, the Cherokee shake white pine sprigs to all the directions. In the Propitiation Festival they sing the Great Hoshanah noticed above ("please save us") and purify their dwellings, both important aspects of the Jewish Sukkot observance. Cherokees sanctify the whole town by beating sycamore wands against the eaves of buildings. At the end of Sukkot on the seventh day, Jews make seven circuits about their tabernacle and then beat willow branches against the floor after singing the hosanna.

Hebrew priests of the Temple in Jerusalem carried crystals about their necks called *urim* and *thummim* ("lights" and "protections"). Known as the Perfect Light, these crystals were carried in the breastplate of the Hebrew high-priest. They were consulted on decisions of war and peace and borne into battle as well as used to divine God's will on crucial occasions in a ritual held before the Holy of Holies. Cherokee priests entrusted with carrying their ark took the *ecacate* ("seeing stones") on war parties. At home, they wore the divinatory crystals about their necks and looked to them on the most solemn occasions to foretell the future. At the New Moon Festival, the Cherokee equivalent of the High Holy Days, people approached the priest after purification to discover whether they would live for another year. The priest gazed into his crystal, another name for which is *oolungtsata*. If he saw the supplicant's figure upright they would live. It the shape was cloudy, they may fall sick, if broken, they may be injured, and if prostrate, they would die before the next New Moon Festival. The alternative name of the divining crystal seems to be Ionic Greek, from the aorist participle for the verb *oulo* "to be well," used in the same sense as the Latin salutation *salve*.

Finally, like the ancient Romans and Greeks and Jewish people with their *mikve*, the Cherokee of old set great store in ritual bathing. They were so fond of "going to water" (*amo': hi atsv': sdi*) that they have even been called "hydrocentric." The ethnographer Raymond Fogelson describes it as the national passion and says it was so ingrained that Christian missionaries had to select another word to translate "baptism," *agawo':da*, meaning "washed clean."

9 THE POSSUM CREEK STONE

What we know is not much
What we do not know is immense.
—Pierre-Simon Laplace

THE peculiar characters of Cherokee script are conventionally attributed to Sequoyah, making him the only person in history to single-handedly invent a system of writing. It seems impious to doubt the story, which is engrained in American memory and tribal pride. But there is evidence Sequoyah did not invent it.

According to rock-art experts, the state of Kentucky possesses the largest number of sites within the entire Ohio River valley. A cave entrance overlooking the Redbird River, a tributary of the South Fork of the Kentucky River in Clay County, Kentucky in the Daniel Boone National Forest, harbors some of these little-known bits of American history. They are part of the extensive Red Bird River Petroglyph Site. A nearby cave is identified as the burial place of a Cherokee man known as Red Bird, also called Aaron Brock. The style of pervasive "well-preserved linear carvings" on flat, vertical sandstone surfaces is "different from any of the previously reported Kentucky petroglyphs," write the authors of the guide published by the Kentucky Heritage Council and State Historic Preservation Office.

Kenneth B. Tankersley of the University of Cincinnati believes our cave entrance "carvings" display a nineteenth-century example of writing in the Cherokee syllabary. "The earliest writing in the system developed by the Cherokee known as Sequoyah, has been found in a

Kentucky cave," announced accordingly the Archaeological Institute of America. Tankersley told *The New York Times* the linear incisions consist of fifteen Cherokee characters and dated them 1818 "or 1808," but they "don't spell any words—they read like ABCs."

Testing of the Y chromosome DNA type of a male claiming descent from Aaron Brock reveals Brock, or Red Bird, together with all his forefathers, apparently carried the Cohen Modal Haplotype. This is the genetic signature of Biblical priests going back to the Jewish patriarch Aaron. The Brock descendant who tested his DNA is J12f2.1+, an ancient form of the Cohen haplotype, which mutates over time (the plus-sign stands for one-step mutations). Chief Red Bird's Y chromosome is not matched in exact particulars by males living in Europe or the Middle East or from families originating there, only by other Cherokees. Since his father, from whom he received his Y chromosome, was a tribally identified Cherokee born about 1700, the appearance of the Cohen Modal Haplotype in America would appear to exclude the possibility Red Bird was the son of English, French, Spanish or Portuguese Jewish settlers. As we have seen, the first European to marry a Cherokee was Cornelius Dougherty. Most intermarriage occurs after 1750.

Chief Red Bird's mother is unquestionably Cherokee, reportedly Paint Clan. Marriage and naming patterns are consistent with Cornell, Sizemore and other Jewish Cherokee or Melungeon or Black Dutch families. The paternal line of this rare Cherokee Kohane can be traced in historical and genealogical records back to Moytoy I, born about 1640. He married Quatsi (Patsy) of Tellico, a fullblood Cherokee of the Wolf Clan. Before 1680, the Cherokee had little contact with Europeans, so it is unlikely Moytoy's father was a European. If he had been, it seems strange that he or his male descendants would have been promoted into positions of leadership in the tribe. His line includes Moytoy II, Red Bird, Raven of Hiwassee, Tathtowe, Bad Water, Old Hop, Old Tassel, Doublehead, Tuckahoe and other Cherokee chiefs. Although most male Cherokee pedigrees were extinguished through warfare following European contact, the survival of the Red Bird or Moytoy line in Brock Y chromosomal DNA is an exception.

Part of the Red Bird rock-art group called Marked Rock has been preserved in Rawlings-Stinson City Park in Manchester since 1994, when a 60-ton chunk of sandstone cliff collapsed on the hillside and fell onto Kentucky State Highway 66. While in place, it was listed as 89001183 on the National Register of Historic Places and marked with a plaque by the Kentucky Historical Society. There are allegedly inscriptions in Old Arabic, or South Semitic, and ogam covering it and scattered elsewhere in the area, in our cave in particular. The Red Bird Petroglyphs lie on the ancient, heavily-traveled Great Warrior Path of the Cherokee that is an extension the Natchez and Avery Trace in Tennessee running north up the Appalachian Mountain chain to the lands of the Iroquois. It was a much-trafficked spot.

A local resident calls our cave entrance inscription Christian Monogram #2 and dates it to the 1st to 2nd cent. CE. He reads, in Greek letters, and translates: *The Savior, Jesus, Son of God the Father, lives.* Though this reading is unsatisfactory for a number of reasons, the language may have been correctly identified. We have sent it round and received several expert opinions. It "could very well indeed be Greek," writes Klaus Hallof, who heads a project of the Berlin Academy of Sciences to publish all the inscriptions of ancient Greece. "We think we can discern the word TOPOS. That suits the context extremely well in that it means, 'This is the place of ....' It would be expected that there would also be a name above TOPOS in the genitive case. TOPOS inscriptions are a widespread occurrence in Greek epigraphy. According to the letter forms (sigma has the long form), the inscription belongs in high or late Augustan times, i.e. 2nd-3rd century after Christ."

Many people miss the fact that there are *two* inscriptions here, not just one. The top line is of one age and character—Greek, not Cherokee—and the bottom line is of an older age and different alphabet, unquestionably Semitic. The letter-forms of the Semitic alphabet resemble the proto-Hebrew script on Maccabee coins. As we saw in the last chapter, several of these coins have been found in the region. Some were struck in honor of Simeon Bar Kochba, the Jewish hero who led the revolt against Roman rule during the reign of Hadrian in 132-35 CE.

Both inscriptions come long before Sequoyah (b. *ca.* 1770) or Red Bird or Aaron Brock. Evaluations by epigraphers place their Greek and Hebrew in the 1st to 3rd cent. CE. The engraving, furthermore, was produced with metal scalpra and maul, whence its striking appearance.

If Greek cannot be Cherokee, could Cherokee be Greek? We pose this question because of another inscription, the Possum Creek Stone. "It was first reported to me in January 1975," writes Gloria Farley, "by Elaine Flud and her friend Jeanna James, who had slipped and fallen over it near the creek bed. It lay at the edge of the old main channel of

Possum Creek, a tributary to Brazeal Creek, the Poteau River and the Arkansas River, near the town of Calhoun. The exact location was 200 yards to the NW of the center of the SW quarter of Section 5, Township 7 North, Range 24 East, Le Flore County, Oklahoma." She adds, "The Possum Creek stone is pecked with four eroded symbols, 3-1/2 to 6 inches tall. They are in a straight line and have mostly curved lines, which is not typical of most inscriptions. The flat stone measures 5 feet long, 30 inches wide, about 5 inches thick, and weighs about 300 pounds."

Gloria shared her discovery with Barry Fell of Harvard University. Fell agreed that the writing was Cherokee and classified it with other ancient East Mediterranean syllabaries like Linear A and Linear B and certain Cypriot scripts. He read the inscription as saying, "Place of Invocation"—an inspired guess, as it turns out. "The discovery of a carved stone in my own Le Flore County, Oklahoma," writes Farley in volume two of *In Plain Sight*, "led me to an in-depth study of Sequoyah, the Cherokee genius, who is believed by most people to have invented the Cherokee syllabary." She goes on to investigate the historical figure known as Sequoyah and conclude that he was really a fictitious person to whom a pre-existing writing system was conveniently, and politically, attributed. She stops at transliterating the inscription or translating it. That is done for the first time by me in this book. The stone is in the collection of the Robert S. Kerr Museum in Poteau, Oklahoma.

The four letters etched in relief on this monumental inscription are, as Farley and Fell recognize, identical to Sequoyah's syllabary. Farley reads SO-NI-WI- SA, and Brian Wilkes, a Cherokee language expert, KE-NI-WI-SA (or HO-NI-KA-SA or LUN-NI-O-SA). None of these readings makes any sense in the Cherokee language. If we read the inscription as Greek, however, it clearly says HO-NI-KA-SA, i.e. "This is the one who has taken the prize of victory." This is a common formula for the inscription on a dais upon which victors are crowned at ancient games. The use is Homeric, although the spelling is Doric, not Ionic (the main dialect found in Homer). The proportions, size and type of inscription on the Possum Creek Stone approximate those of a number of ancient Greek victory altars or victor's pedestals. A good example of one in Greece's National Archeological Museum comes from Athens and dates to the 5th century BCE.

Cherokee writing, then, does not appear to be the invention of Sequoyah but represents an ancient East Mediterranean script similar to Linear A, Linear B and other Cypriot and Minoan syllabaries. Only one other sample of ancient Cherokee epigraphy has been reported: a brief inscription in Cherokee characters published in the *Jefferson* (N.C.) *Times* newspaper in June of 1983. It is likely that more will be found once people know what to look for. The two known examples are both pre-Columbian and prove that the Cherokee writing system was practiced before Sequoyah in Oklahoma and North Carolina.

A different account of the syllabary emerges in Traveller Bird's *Tell Them They Lie*. Published in 1971, it is a curious book. Without citing any evidence, and in fact, defiantly refusing to do so, Traveller Bird makes several unusual claims. First, the Sequoyah of the history books never existed, only a man named George Guess (1766-1839) or Sogwali (Horse), warrior-scribe of his people. Sequoyah's true father was not Christopher Gist/Guess, or as others would have it, a German peddler, but Young Warrior (Gvlihuanida) of Sogwiligigagei (Red Horse Place, now in Rutherford County, North Carolina). Sequoyah did not invent the syllabary associated with his name. It had been used by the Cherokee (whom he calls Talagi) since 1483 and before. In other words, it was not devised from English, Hebrew and German letterforms in the years between 1809 and 1822, as frequently claimed. Finally, there was never any painting of Sequoyah, or George Guess, or George Gist, because the true Sequoyah had been disfigured. The famous portrait by McKenney is of Thomas Maw.

Traveller Bird obviously has an animus that colors his work. He calls the white traders "traitors," and the Indians "red sons-of-bitches." He lambasts "sainthood stories" and "made-up information" about Sequoyah at every turn. But is Traveller Bird's biography any "truer" than the versions he attacks? As scholars point out, there are as many Sequoyahs as there are biographers. Neither his parentage nor birth date seems to be known with certainty. The famous letter to the U.S. government reporting his mysterious death while in Mexico on the trail of lost Cherokee, it has recently been suggested, was a forgery.

Most other sources on Sequoyah contradict Traveller Bird. For instance, "The Life of George Gist" was dictated to John Howard Payne in 1835 by Major George Lowrey, Sequoyah's cousin; Mike Waters, Sequoyah's brother-in-law; and The Bark, another relative associated with Sequoyah since his youth. In it, Gist's age is given as about 60 and he is said to have left the Cherokee Nation with the Arkansas emigrants about eleven years before. In 1843, he was reported to have died on a trip undertaken on behalf of the tribe in San

Fernando, Tamaulipas, Mexico. A Sequoyah descendant, Molly Running Wolf, maintains that the place of Sequoyah's death is a town called San Fernando just south of San Miguel de Allende, and that there are "blond-haired, blue-eyed Cherokee" of the family name De Luna living there at present.

One detail of Traveller Bird's account does ring true. According to him, Sequoyah's people came from the West and after encounters with the Americans returned to the West. An origin in the West explains the location of the Possum Creek stone in Oklahoma, while the return of the Keetoowah to the same area provides the reason for the United Keetoowah Band's presence across the Mississippi today. When one of Constantine Rafinesque's friends, naturalist Thomas Nuttall, visited them in 1819, the Keetoowah were already partially removed and living in Arkansas. In fact, Chief Beverly Northrop maintains they were present in the Old Louisiana Territory since 1721, and perhaps before that, as Lost Cherokees. The Possum Creek stone was found just where we would expect to find it considering the Eshelokee's migrations through Oklahoma and Arkansas.

From family records and the John Howard Payne papers, we get a coherent biography of the Sequoyah who was the son of Cherokee trader Nathaniel Gist. Perhaps the conflicting accounts can be reconciled if there *were* actually two persons who went by that name, a scribe-warrior and the half-breed son of the trader. Proof of the latter's existence is in the form of a letter preserved by the Gist family stating that Sequoyah visited his father Nathaniel Gist in Kentucky and was acknowledged as his natural son. Whatever the solution, it is evident that the "Sequoyan" syllabary greatly predates its alleged modern inventor. Despite what Traveller Bird says, it goes back far beyond 1483.

Mention of the Lunas and Gists brings us again to Sephardim. Both are Crypto-Jewish families. Sequoyah's parentage is another instance of a Jewish trader marrying the daughter of a Cherokee chief. His mother is Wurteh (Gurty or Gerty, a diminutive of Margaret). A contemporary of his father is the Virginian Samuel Gist, partner of George Washington. Samuel Gist became one of the first admiralty insurance brokers in London. He lived for nearly a hundred years, helped start Lloyd's Bank of London and owned the first stud racehorse to come to America, an "Arabian Turk." The horse, Bulle Rocke, was foaled about 1718, and out of him sprang some of the most valuable of U.S. racing stock. In *The Fabulous History of the Dismal*

Swamp Company, Gist is explicitly called "an old Jew" by son-in-law John Anderson. By blood or marriage, he was related to the Smiths, Andersons, Coopers, Ashleys (Arabic and Hebrew for "honey seller"), Howards (dukes of Norfolk, originally *Norman* Hereward "guards of the Army"), Boleyn/Bollings (Hebrew "bath keeper"), and Masseys (from Sephardic surname Mazza), an Edinburgh and Aberdeen mercantile family. There is a small town on Sand Mountain, a Melungeon-populated place, named Guess, and when Joseph Gist died, his manumitted slaves were granted land in Ohio. They went there *en masse*, becoming the so-called Brown County Melungeons.

The origin of the Gist surname seems to be Altaic Turkic GOSTATA, the name of a line of Khazar rulers in the Caucasus who adopt Judaism after holding a contest between the three major religions. Its Byzantine form is KOSTAS. The same dynasty later spearheads a migration of Khazar converts to Kiev and the Ukraine, where their name is rendered in Latin letters as *Gostou-n/s*. In Spain, the family adopts the name Da Costa, which they derived from "God's rib" (Hebrew Abravanel). Acosta is a variant. This becomes Kist in Ashkenaz (*Ger.* "coast," through a pun on *costa*, which can mean either "rib" or "coast"). From all accounts, then, it appears that the Da Costa, Abravanel and Gist families of Spain, Italy, the Low Lands and the British Isles were originally Khazar Turkish converts. The same name occurs in the Ragusan/Croatian/Venetian Gozzi family of traders, explorers, admirals, and physicians active in Elizabethan London and the Ottoman Empire.

Contemporary references to Christopher Gist, Deputy Indian Commissioner to Gov. Edmond Atkin of Maryland, and agent of the Ohio Company, describe him as exceedingly tall, dark-complexioned and hairy, with a full beard. George Guess's half-sister, Maria Cecil Gist, married Benjamin Gratz of Lexington, Kentucky (1792-1884), son of the frontier merchant Michael Gratz who endowed the Spanish and Portuguese synagogues in Philadelphia and New York and established communities in Lancaster and Lexington. The Gratz family came to Philadelphia from Inquisitorial Spain, where their name was Gracia, or Garcia, via Silesia. They intermarried with the Hayses, Howards, Frankses, Ettings and Levys.

Could these roots explain why the portrait of George Guess, or Sequoyah, shows him in a Turkish turban and distinctly Mediterranean clothing? And why he was a silversmith, a rare occupation for an American Indian at that time?

Both the Red Bird inscriptions and Possum Creek Stone offer solid evidence for the Greek origins of the Cherokee. Together with the syllabary's connections with Phoenician tablets and the Cherokee's discarded base-five Meso-American numbering system, the rock-art record captures the trail of the Eshelokee from South America through Mexico to Arkansas and Tennessee. In all the locations where they have resided and settled and migrated, Cherokee have welcomed Sephardic Jews into their society.

10 RISING FROM THE FLAMES

There are many humorous things in the world, among them the
white man's notion that he is less savage than the other savages.
—Mark Twain

IN Robert Conley's *The Dark Way*, the Ani-Kutani priests are
overthrown by their fellow Cherokee tribesmen, who accuse them,
among other things, of privileged behavior and trying to revive the
ancient practice of human sacrifice. Although the Kutani promise this
act will propitiate the angry spirits and revive the tribe's failing crops,
the other Cherokee men and women rise up against them when a
young warrior returns home and discovers his beautiful wife raped by
one of the priests. The rulers had become "haughty, insolent,
overbearing, and licentious to an intolerable degree." The outraged
people kill every Kutan, young and old. In the aftermath, Cherokee
society takes on a different tenor. The Kutani retreat into the
background, where they remain to this day

We have met these Kutani before. They are Rafinesque's Kutans,
"who came easterly through the Atlantic ocean," Mediterranean
peoples who appear to have spoken Afro-Asiatic or Proto-Pelagian
languages. Their counterparts, the Atlans, who seem to belong to Indo-
European language groups for the most part, settled the hinterlands of
Eastern North America with them, where they built the imposing
mounds at Poverty Point, Newark and other centers. Following the
cataclysms that "interrupted the intercourse between Europe and

America" and left both the Atlans and Kutans to pursue their own course of development, a tribe named as Tsalagi appears on the world stage for the first time. They are heirs of the Atalan civilization, which has gradually disintegrated to produce the Zolacans, as Rafinesque refers to the Cherokee, as well as the Appalachee, Calusa, Conoy and Talegans. During the same period, the Kutans fragment into the Maya, Pawnee, Catawba, Coosa, Cusseta and "Tanasi of Tennessee," the Danaans or Greeks.

We saw how the "Cherokees or Zolucans, an Atlan nation dwelling west of the Mississippi, being driven by the Oghuzians [Algonquian Indians from South Siberia], came to Kentucky and Tennessee, and settled at last after many wars in the mountains of Carolina, where they became a nation of hunting mountaineers." The Cherokee gather up remnants of the Atlan-affiliated Talegans and part company with their old allies in the Ohio Valley, the Lenape, Iroquois and Shawnee. In Tennessee, the fair-skinned Cherokee blend successfully with the Yuchi, Coosa, Catawba and Cusseta—smaller-bodied, Semitic and darker-skinned—while keeping the fierce Asiatic Indians and Northerlys at bay. During the Mississippian Period, a balance of power evolves as the Cherokees amalgamate with southern mound-building Kutan tribes and enjoy on-again, off-again friendly relations with the Natchez and Muscoghean tribes to the south. The next great transformation does not come until they revolt against the Kutan priesthood.

One consequence of the eradication of the Kutans by the Cherokee was that "all religious ceremonies" and "priestly functions" were "assumed thereafter by individual doctors and conjurors." Another was that any unified political organization they may have had before that now fell apart.

We do not know for sure when this ethnic cleansing took place—Chief John Ross thought it occurred in the early eighteenth century and Adair places it in a similar time frame—but clearly, it had enormous repercussions for the Cherokee people.

In the absence of much to go on, most historians and anthropologists assume that the Cherokee were like other Indians of the region and had no central government to speak of. Raymond Fogelson in his article on the Cherokee in the *Handbook of American Indians* writes:

> Although they constituted a people with a shared language and culture, the Cherokees could hardly be regarded

as a tribe, in the sense of a unified polity with superordinate system of authority, until the mid-nineteenth century, when pressure from the Americans forced the establishment of a unified government.

The narrative outlined by William McLoughlin in his book *Cherokee Renascence in the New Republic* tells the story of halting and confused acquiescence to the overtures of U.S. presidents Jefferson, Madison, Adams and Jackson. When the National Council in New Echota finally passes legislation establishing a "new republic," McLoughlin claims, the laws simply "overlay aspects of Anglo-Saxon jurisprudence on Cherokee customs." This move "risked alienating [a] conservative people in order to prove to the white man that the Cherokees could understand and manage a republican form of government...and [had] considerable appeal to the missionaries whom the Cherokees were eager to have on their side." Such framing with little credit given to Indians for their own contributions to a synthesis or process of acculturation is common among U.S. academic historians.

In reality, it was probably Jewish merchants like the Coopers and Gists who first nudged the Cherokee into nation building, not New England Christians. Both Jews and Indians had a lot in common. Some of the Indians' ancient Greek and Egyptian institutions from their long Kutan and Atlan pasts may have still been in makeshift operation. We have seen how the Eshelokee added a decidedly Greek tone to Cherokee life. More importantly, though, the Cherokee, like their neighbors the Creeks, absorbed a large infusion of Muslim customs. At the time of contact with the English and Americans, there were upwards of eighty-five Cherokee towns. Each had its own Greek-styled assembly hall and Muslim-styled police force. As a city of refuge, Chota fulfilled the same role as Delphi or Jerusalem, although not a political capital until the Jewish traders made it one. The towns were only loosely confederated, in the fashion of Greek city-states. Outside them were bands of Cherokees under leaders who behaved much like independent sheiks. Out of this ancient and multi-layered system, arriving Jewish and Crypto-Jewish traders, interpreters and agents forged an office of "principal chief" for treaty-signing purposes. They were America's earliest diplomats to conquered peoples. Even before the Cherokee Nation was fitted out with all the accoutrements of sovereignty, indeed before it existed on paper, it had representatives at large in Charleston, Pensacola, Philadelphia, New York, Havana, Amsterdam and London.

Muslim traders appear to have been very active on American shores. Al-Masudi's *Historical Annals* of 942 C.E. records a sea voyage when a ship under the command of Captain Khashkhash (probably a Babylonian) set sail from Cordova, Spain. After a long journey west across the Atlantic, it returned laden with treasures. Al-Idrisi in his world geography, *Nuzhet al-Mushtag* (1154), tells of a similar voyage undertaken by the Brothers Al-Mugrurim who embarked from Lisbon seeking islands in the western Atlantic. They sailed for about a month and brought back a report that the opposite lands were inhabited by Berbers and thick with sheep. Over the centuries, Arab-speaking visitors or settlers seem to have penetrated far into the interior. Islamic coins, Arabic trade tokens and Kufic writing remain as the signs of their activities from Massachusetts to Tennessee.

The Kutans, as we have seen, had deep roots in North Africa. Islamic scholar Ivan Van Sertima refers to a thesis published by the French commandant Jules Cauvet in Algiers in the 1930s, who examined the origins of seventy-seven tribes on both sides of the Atlantic. One example is the Guales of South Carolina, who appear to be the same as the Guellaïa of the Rif in North Africa. The North African origins of the Coree are also noteworthy. Colonization efforts evidently also went in the opposite direction. A study by the anthropologist Harold Lawrence appearing in 1962 demonstrates that certain tribes living in the Sahara possess American Indian traits with similar names and naming methods. The Berber "Indians" live in tents rather than the mud-brick houses of their neighbors.

Of all sites in North America, Tennessee has the best-known and longest inscriptions in Kufic Arabic writing. According to Barry Fell, Arab traders in the Southeast contributed the core vocabulary to the language we now call Mobilian Trade Jargon. As well as providing the basic form of intertribal commercial contract and system of credit, the *commenda*, Islamic institutions also played a role in the development of civil administration and military organization for Indian tribes. Jewish and Muslim models of civic life from the world of the Mediterranean and Near East comingle. These models were fundamentally different from the feudalism of Northern Europe brought over by the British and French.

Cherokee chieftains living in the hills and hollows away from townlife very much evoke Muslim *shaykhs*. In the words of Albert

Hourani, an Arab historian, these are de facto leaders who "had little effective power except that which was given them by their reputation in the public opinion of the group." The British found it exasperating to deal with their equivalents among the Indians. Some bands were so furtive they even escaped the dragnet of removal that came later with the Americans. Tsali and his tribesmen in North Carolina held out defiantly after the Trail of Tears and their group eventually became the Eastern Band of Cherokee Indians. A multitude of other Eastern and Southeastern Indian groups are still fighting today for federal recognition.

In a Cherokee town, just as in Islam, there existed structured government, a developed administrative system and a sense of history and cultural traditions. Its leaders were military officials in the mold of dynastic rulers administering Muslim cities, the *sayyids* or *sharifs*. These descendants of the Prophet ran the affairs of the *shari'a*, assuring implementation of a social code in compliance with the dictates of religion, in exactly the same role played by the Kutan priesthood. Likewise, the government of the Cherokee state was essentially military in nature, with a caste of headmen given titles that were martial in origin. Like Muslim appointees, members of this elite corps moved between towns as governors. The same Crypto-Jewish half-breed families held control of the Cherokee state from its formal beginnings until its extinction in 1900. After that, the U.S. government dissolved tribal government and allotted communal land in severalty under the Dawes Act. But the age-old patterns of public life continued. There has always been constant friction between admixed town-dwellers with their wealth and guarantees of law and order and the mostly full-blood country folk with their clan system and notions of summary justice.

The ancient office of *qadi* is peculiar to Arabs and their neighbors. The word itself probably has the same root as the name Ani-Kutani, and it too finds an echo in Cherokee society. As Hourani describes it, the *qadi* represents the urban elite placed in charge of guarding "a system of learning, values, modes of behavior and ideal types of personality." A similar function is performed by the Keetoowah and Seven Scribes' Society of the Cherokee. In the acculturation process, these traditional roles are gradually usurped, and improved upon, by the half-breeds. The mixed bloods rekindle a public-spirited model inspired by the Islamic idea of the *waqf*, or foundation, for the property-less. In the Muslim world, the *waqf* is "an assignment in perpetuity of the income from a piece of property for charitable purposes, for example, the maintenance of mosques, schools, hospitals, public fountains or hostels for travellers, the freeing of prisoners, or the care of sick animals. It could also be used, however, for the benefit of the founder's family." In this same spirit, the Vanns endowed the Moravian school at Spring Place, where they had their own children and relatives educated. It was the same story at the Brainerd Mission at Creek Path. Doublehead and others established large plantations along the same principles. On Sand Mountain, the Burns, Lowrey and Davis families even sought a special section of land from the U.S. government to build a self-sustaining college.

Many of these Arab-styled leaders among the Cherokee belonged to the Deer Clan, the third of the original clans. Deer Clan members were supposed to be good intellects. Anawaika or Deerhead Cove at the foot of Fox Mountain between northern Georgia and Alabama, near Lookout Mountain, was one of their traditional territories. Part of Paint-town in North Carolina was once called Deer Place. The Cherokee clans were suppressed by the reforms of affluent half-breed planters and Deer Clan members and brought under a new judicial system. The Light Horse Brigade introduced by Maj. Ridge (al-Wadi) is, unsurprisingly, modeled on the institution of the *qadi*. Henceforth, Cherokee marshals, not clans, had the power to punish acts like illicit sexual intercourse, theft, drunkenness and murder.

A formal decree abolishing clan law was signed at Eustanala, April 18, 1810, "by order of the seven clans." A reactionary Ghost Dance Movement flared up briefly in 1811, but by the time of removal in 1838, clans were little more than a memory. Government rolls largely ignored them, emphasizing patriarchal credentials and father's surname rather than mothers and female-linked relationships. Marriage within one's clan, formerly punishable by death, eventually became a non-issue. Probably few Cherokee today can recite the clan history of their parents and forebears with any great degree of confidence. Descendants with minor amounts of Cherokee blood, even those who may preserve a direct female line, are often completely in the dark.

When they resettle in Oklahoma, the Cherokee seek to transplant many of these ancient institutions. The same leading families help found orphanages, schools, libraries, assembly halls, stomp grounds and even interest-free lender banks. In more than one respect, the Cherokee at the time were far in advance of the rest of American society. Whether they knew it or not, they emulated Marrano ideals of community. Jewish history is replete with the stories of Sephardim who establish their own "nations" in exile after 1492. Typically, as in the case of Livorno, Bayonne, New Amsterdam, Savannah and the Caribbean islands, the parnassim or leaders move quickly to set up a widows' pension fund, orphanage, cemetery society and other charitable organizations.

Let us turn now to external relations in the new Cherokee state. Whereas the old model of treaty making revolved around notions of kinship, with Indians addressing colonists as "our brothers" and the English or French king as "our father," the new leaders around 1790 adopt an approach based on egalitarian principles in negotiating with the white man. Thanks to Attakullakulla (who calls himself "president," not "chief"), Nancy Ward, Trader John MacDonald and Chief John Ross, the Cherokee are often able to treat with Washington on a parity. Undoubtedly, this strategy stemmed from the counsel of half-breeds of Portuguese Jewish or Scottish Jewish extraction. Suddenly, the Echota chiefs begin to deliver written copies of their "talks," a practice unparalleled in any other Indian tribe. These expanded charters and dispatches developed a notion of justice and just relations. And they acted as a durable record for arguments that might otherwise be swept aside and ignored. The half-Sephardic Oconostota even wrote letters to the editor of the Knoxville Gazette published after his death in 1792, if we are to credit one account. Eventually, the Cherokee were able to send embassies to Washington City, hire lawyers and accountants and retain lobbyists for their cause.

At the center of all these developments are the Ridges, Lowreys, Waties, Hickses and Rosses. Elias Boudinot (1800-1838), first editor of *The Phoenix* newspaper, was actually the brother of Stand Watie. Known originally as Buck Watie (Gallegina), he took his name from Elias Boudinot, the Yankee lawyer who served as the first president of the Continental Congress. The elder Elias Boudinot wrote *Star in the West,* an exposition of the Lost Tribes of Israel theory about American Indians. The *Cherokee Phoenix* was published in English and Cherokee from 1828 until 1834. As evident from its first issues, its overriding purpose was political: to unite Cherokees scattered in isolated pockets across eight different states in the East and four in the West. The first number contained the Constitution of the Cherokee Nation along with a proud display of Sequoyah's syllabary.

The symbol chosen for the national newspaper was an image of the phoenix, a fabulous beast from Greek folklore and Jewish mysticism. Prehistoric Cherokee have many stories about this mythic bird. It was said to be the largest in the world. Adair gives its name as Sinnawah, although others call it Tlanuwa, Tsalnuwah or Tlaniwa the "Great Hawk." Adair's rendering of the name seems to be the original form. Taking a broad view, the Cherokee phoenix is the same as the Sina, or Saena, of Persian stories, S'yena in Sanskrit, all of which mean "raptor," as does Cherokee *tlanu*, "swoop down." The fabulous Senmurw (Saena Bird) was known to all peoples of the Middle East. It is the basis of the Arab people's roc, phoenix of Greek legend and Simorgh ("Sina-bird") of Judeo-Persian folktales.

The symbol of the phoenix served Marranos in Amsterdam, Livorno and Salonika as an emblem of state. True to its meaning in both Cherokee and Jewish usage, it stood for the resurrected spirit of a chosen people. Portuguese Jews went by the name "gentes de naçao," People of the Nation. Although they paid lip service to their Portuguese citizenship, their secret meaning of the term was the Hebrew Nation. A Judeo-Spanish prayer book of 1612 displays the phoenix as the special badge for the Amsterdam congregation Neve Salom, with the Hebrew verse "Who is like thee?" (Ex. 15:11).

The case of Euchella v. Welsh in 1824 represented an ambitious bid by intermarried Jewish landowners to create a national reservation for the Cherokee in the East. Like the Phoenix newspaper, it would mark the Cherokees' arrival into an elite circle. Soon there was talk they might receive a seat in Congress. Public sympathy for them was fanned to new intensity by converted Jews like John Howard Payne. In the end, they never won the promised representation in Washington. But they did secure a permanent place in the story of America.

The Cherokee nation was inspired by and patterned on the Sephardic experience, but it has never been Zionistic. It was born as a nation in exile. The full meaning of exile would become plain when the Cherokee, after being driven out of Tennessee into Georgia, were removed to Arkansas, then to Oklahoma, and when even these lands were taken from them. The Cherokee Nation, like world Jewry, has been repeatedly destroyed. But in the process, it has always risen again like the phoenix. The ancient heritage of the Ani-Kutani could not be laid to rest as easily as story and song might have it.

EPILOG

Who can tell the dancer from the dance?
—William Butler Yeats

IT is no accident that key pieces of the puzzle proving Greek, Libyan, Egyptian, Jewish and Berber settlement in ancient native America have been forgotten. In 2006, word reached me that the Los Lunas Decalogue Stone was vandalized. The alleged Phoenician version of the Ten Commandments on a boulder in the Isleta Indian Reservation in New Mexico was defaced by someone who took a hammer to it and marred the top two lines of Hebrew writing, including the name of God. These acts of destruction are very thorough and deliberate. We lose a little of our national cultural patrimony every time such things happen. The closing of minds in their aftermath often is hermetic and final.

The proofs and refutations of history frequently hang by slender threads. On excellent authority, Constantine Rafinesque showed that the first inhabitants of North America came from Europe, the Mediterranean and Middle East. The Americas underwent a transition to town life and agricultural production not unlike the rest of the world. Yet on the basis of two anthropologists' articles, Rafinesque's history is categorically rejected today.

In my opinion, the genetic story of the Americas has been botched. Not only are samples flawed but geneticists' times to coalescence are forced into the Procrustean bed of outdated theory.

Many haplogroups are ignored, while haplotypes and genealogies are never investigated.

There is a reason why Columbus and other explorers called the natives they discovered savages. That word applied originally to those who had been cut off and reduced to a primitive condition. Evidently, Arabs, Romans, Jews and others who came to the shores of America recognized people who were their own.

American history is usually presented as a clash between Old and New World cultures. There is room in the textbooks for only one "peopling," one discovery, one *entrada*. It's Them vs. Us. As we learn more, though, the Christian colonial powers had their own Indians at home, in pagan Europeans, Irish, Saracens and others they had vanquished before setting out for the Western Hemisphere. The "Indians" over here already had European, North African and Middle Eastern connections. The shock of recognition went both ways. The saga of America's melting pot takes on a different meaning if we emphasize similarities rather than differences and study all the instances of trade, cooperation, intermarriage and interchange of ideas.

The Cherokee are the largest Indian nation in the U.S., and for that matter, the world. They lay claim to the longest continuity of any people outside India and China, older than the Greeks, Romans, Jews, Egyptians, Persians, Turks, Arabs and any European country. It is ironic that they turn out to have significant Greek and Jewish roots. Greco-Roman civilization and Judeo-Christian ideas and traditions are seen as high points in man's cultural achievements. This type of idealization has normally been denied to Native Americans, who are perceived as fundamentally un-European, un-modern, un-progressive. With a fresh look, perhaps some of the same qualities we admire in Greek philosophers and heroes of the Bible can now be glimpsed in American Indians and their descendants.

If the Cherokee followed Judaism before the arrival of Protestant missionaries, and this was not due to the influence of Jewish traders, they practiced an ancient form of it. Their public and private observance of Judaic law was never subjected to the persecutions and disturbances suffered by European Jewry. Mixed with other elements, it was, to judge from eighteenth century observers, part of the state religion. Modern-day Jews can perhaps derive a sense of pride from its unexpected survival on the opposite side of the globe from Jerusalem.

I have been not only surprised but also a little sorry to have arrived at the conclusions I was forced to draw from this personal odyssey. I wish it had been otherwise. I wish that my Cherokee ancestors had turned out to be the numinous figures I admired from tales and textbooks, that their original homeland had ever been the Great Smoky Mountains, where my family vacationed, and that they were by nature a people who turned away from the allurements of technology, physical comfort and material gain to embrace a life of spirituality and earthy contentment. The reality is that they were more like ancient Greeks, Egyptians and Jews, the acknowledged founders of modern Western civilization. This is not to rob them of any mystery. It should make us feel closer and more akin to each other, and it should invite an explosion of new studies. I hope it is the beginning of a more nuanced understanding of our common mysteries, our common diversity and the factors that have made the Cherokees one of the most enduring of all peoples. The ancient Greeks, Phoenicians, Israelites and Egyptians are gone.

The Cherokees remain.

ABOUT THE AUTHOR

DONALD Yates was born in Cedartown, Georgia. He attended Stetson University, University of Vienna, University of Freiburg, Duke University and University of North Carolina at Chapel Hill, where he earned a Ph.D. in classical studies with a concentration on Medieval Latin Studies. His books include *The Bear Went over the Mountain, Los Lunas Decalogue Stone* and *Old World Roots of the Cherokee*. With Elizabeth C. Hirschman, he authored *The Early Jews and Muslims of England and Wales: A Genetic and Genealogical History*. With Phyllis E. Starnes he recently published *Ancestors and Enemies: Essays on Melungeons*. He lives in Phoenix.

Made in United States
Troutdale, OR
12/06/2024